PEAK PERFORMANCE
for SMART KIDS

PEAK PERFORMANCE
for SMART KIDS

*Strategies and Tips
for Ensuring School Success*

Maureen Neihart, Psy.D.

Routledge
Taylor & Francis Group

NEW YORK AND LONDON

First published in 2008 by Prufrock Press Inc.

Published in 2021 by Routledge
605 Third Avenue, New York, NY 10017
4 Park Square, Milton Park, Abingdon, Oxon OX14 4RN

Routledge is an imprint of the Taylor & Francis Group, an informa business

Library of Congress Cataloging-in-Publication Data

Neihart, Maureen.
  Peak performance for smart kids : strategies and tips for ensuring school success / by Maureen Neihart.
    p. cm.
  Includes bibliographical references.
  ISBN 978-1-59363-310-3 (pbk.)
  1. Gifted children—Education 2. Learning—Psychology of. 3. Education—Parent participation. I. Title.
  LC3993.N45 2008
  371.95'6--dc22
                        2008006925

ISBN 13: 978-1-59363-310-3 (pbk)

DOI: 10.4324/9781003237068

Contents

Contents

Foreword

AS I was browsing through the manuscript of this wonderful book by psychologist Maureen Neihart, my elder son Zhong had just returned from a mountain climbing trip to Mount Kinabalu. Zhong will begin his first year at university doing a double degree in law and economics, but for now, before his term begins, he is set on adventure. A family friend met my wife and I just a few days before Zhong returned and were shocked that we allowed him to travel alone to Kota Kinabalu and attempt the ascent. At nearly 4,100 meters, Mount Kinabalu is the highest mountain in Borneo, and all of Southeast Asia. Like all parents we too had our concerns but understood that he needed to venture out on his own—as Maureen describes in her book, "out of the comfort zone . . . to the edge of their competence." My younger son Chen was just released from his first 2 weeks of military service that very same evening while I was reading this book. He came back in his smart military uniform and was immediately off to the gym. He used to write his own goals—50 push-ups, 30 bicep curls of 15-pound weights, and so forth—that have transformed his physique, not to mention his confidence and esteem.

Maureen's book caused me to reflect on the times when my sons were very frail kids struggling to achieve their various aspirations in their primary school and teenage days. Zhong was a national squash trainee when he was at Raffles Institution and recently, while still with the military service, he also represented his division in the Armed Forces—they came out tops. I remember the many times he was anxious and at times frustrated when honing his squash skills as a teenager. Our culture celebrates talent and has little patience with those who "try too hard." It does not appreciate that sport, like any academic subject, challenges those who attempt it with a steep learning curve, yet is ultimately rewarding and a source of validation for a young person. When Zhong was 15, we were so concerned about how he was coping with his studies (as his grades in school were alarming), that we had to write him a note lamenting our concerns. Two years ago he achieved straight distinctions in his A Level Examinations, including one in economics, a subject he pursued with an interest that took him beyond the boundaries of any syllabus.

My younger son Chen used to write some of the saddest entries in his diary in primary school—he was classified as "unable to read" in his first grade and placed with the learning support group. But, like all parents who spend enough time with our children, we knew our kids better than any diagnostic system, we knew they had abilities and that they could reach their peak performance some day. We just wanted to ensure that they be given opportunities to explore and fulfill their God-given talents. The school environment is not always so kind, with educators striving to hit the right note between keeping bright students engaged and helping slower students keep up. But, even with opportunities and a good support environment it is never easy out there. They fall down and need to get up and not give up. By the time Chen completed his secondary school years the boy who could not read had become valedictorian and winner of the N. Vaithinathan award for outstanding achievement in all areas; recognized for leadership achievement in the student council, with straight A's in the Cambridge O Level Examinations; and a Gold Medal winner of the Sharma Book prize for language and literature. Maureen is right—many times it is mental resilience and psychological prowess that our children need to develop and discover their potential. For parents, it may be a willingness to take risks, including the risk of faith.

There were many occasions I remember Zhong swinging imaginary forehands and backhands at home, visualizing hypothetical opponents and winning matches, if only in the arena of the mind. His team would watch and review movies like *Remember the Titans* when they were preparing for major tournaments—exactly along the similar vein of mental and emotional preparation that this book recommends. Managing stress, setting smart goals and visualizing success, and identifying positive emotions and getting into the mood with positive optimism—these were the things they truly learned and I cannot agree more with Maureen that the most important thing is that my children did what they loved to do and had the opportunities to reach and build small success experiences. Maureen captures in her book some of the things that upon reflection I really wished I had known earlier as a parent without having to undertake so many trial-and-error approaches!

Now speaking as an academic, psychologist, and researcher, I want to congratulate Maureen for her efforts in putting together a very well-researched work. We have too many books of this sort that are technical, dry, and uninspired. She has in many ways succeeded in crystallizing the best insights from the dense literature of psychology, coupled with practical wisdom for nurturing peak performance. She also has articulated these in a way that is highly accessible, readable, and engaging with many interesting case examples and excellent practical pointers.

I strongly recommend this book to parents, educators, and psychologists interested in helping the young and the next generation achieve their peak performance in school, extracurricular activities, and life.

Oon-Seng Tan, Ph.D.
Head of Psychological Studies, National Institute of
Education, Singapore
President-Elect, Asia-Pacific Educational Research Association

What Do Coaches, Athletes, and Performing Artists Know That We Don't?

IN my 30 years of working with talented children and their families, I have met many capable children who struggled to realize their promise. The challenges they faced often were not due to their lack of motivation or to lack of support from their parents. The difficulties they had were common to every child who pursues a passion. They didn't have the mental skills to stay at the top of their game. They didn't know how to play the inner game of high achievement.

No one taught them.

I suspect that there are many more children out there just like them, kids who are talented, eager, and in love with something. Perhaps you're the parent of one. The challenges I've seen other children face may be similar to those you're facing with your children:

She used to really enjoy ice skating, but now . . . there's so much pressure. She can't handle it. It's not fun anymore. She says she wants to do other things.

DOI: 10.4324/9781003237068-1

We've seen big changes since she hit puberty. She's really torn between doing what she loves and doing the things her friends are doing. We hate to see her give up on her dreams.

There's a lot of pressure on boys in our neighborhood. Pressure not to study, to not take school seriously. It's getting harder for him to stay in the accelerated classes. He gets teased a lot.

He does well, but he gets terribly frustrated when things don't come easily. He cries and wants to give up. There are lots of things in life that don't come easily. How can we help him learn to persevere?

His anger gets the best of him when he's stressed. He hasn't learned how to keep his cool.

All of our kids are very motivated to work hard. We're thankful! But it is tough at times to keep up with them all. It's stressful on our family. We don't want to lose our focus on the most important things.

There is a level of achievement at which further talent development takes more than ability and hard work. It requires psychological preparedness—mental and emotional skills that drive performance. Many of the most capable children will eventually fail to realize their potential if no one teaches them the inner game of high achievement.

Psychological preparedness may be the single most neglected component of talent development, even though you and I, and your children's teachers and coaches, would all agree it's a pivotal factor in any achievement.

There are seven mental competencies that drive performance:
- a tolerance for stress or anxiety,
- a willingness to work at the edge of one's competence (risk-taking),
- SMART goal setting,
- mental rehearsal,
- optimism,
- mood management, and
- an ability to resolve the need to belong with the need to achieve.

These are the skills that keep our focus sharp, order our attention, and keep us engaged in the learning process. I call these the seven psychological skills of high performance, or the inner game of high achievement.

They are not innate, but can be trained. If we want to help children realize their potential, we need to be intentional in our efforts to help them learn these mental skills for high performance.

It doesn't matter if your children are 6 or 16, if they love sports or art. Helping them master these seven skills will prepare them to cope with the emotional and mental demands of higher achievement. Mastering these skills for one effort also will help them master them for other challenges ahead.

In the pages that follow we'll examine each of these skills. We'll explore how they contribute to high performance, and we'll have fun doing exercises you can use with your kids. If your children are struggling, this information will provide a detailed blueprint for boosting their performance. If they already are doing very well, this material will help them be able to repeat the best day they've ever had.

Let's take a quick look at each of the seven competencies needed to play the inner game of high achievement. Then, in subsequent chapters, we'll explore each one in more detail, outlining strategies and supports designed to develop them in children.

Competency #1: An Ability to Manage Stress and Anxiety

Fear often gets in the way of high achievement. As competition intensifies and stakes rise, so do stress and anxiety. Children who have no strategies for keeping a lid on their anxiety will not be able to do their best.

Perhaps you believe that America's increased emphasis on high-stakes testing and accountability for academic outcomes has increased children's stress. Whether it has or not, one thing is clear, children who are able to effectively manage their stress, those who can make their stress work *for them*, are going to achieve more.

The relationship between performance and anxiety has many variations within and across individuals. Some people have a very high tolerance for stress, whereas low levels of stress negatively impact others. Stress motivates some people and paralyzes others. Fear causes some people to step back, while for others it interferes with concentration, attention, or motor control.

It doesn't matter how much stress a child feels, or how that stress affects him or her, the steps for learning to keep a lid on anxiety and to maintain it at levels that keep you working hard are the same. It's easy to learn to manage anxiety. It just takes practice. Children simply have to learn how to

- breathe,
- relax, and
- keep moving toward the things that scare them.

These are easy to teach, easy to learn, and with practice, can make an enormous difference in a child's capacity to work hard toward high goals. I'll show you how in Chapter 2.

Competency #2: A Willingness to Work at the Edge of One's Competence

High achievement also requires a willingness to get out of your comfort zone and work at the edge of your competence. A common frustration among parents is children who can but won't. We know that the best learning takes place when children have to reach for their goals and have the supports in place to accomplish their goals. To improve, children must work at a level that requires them to make an effort, and they must work with others who have similar interests, ability, and drive.

This requires risk.

The further a child moves along the trajectory of achievement, the more uncertain outcomes become. It is impossible to go from good to great without taking realistic risks, without a willingness to move out of one's comfort zone toward the edge of competence.

Understanding the relationship between risk taking and achievement, and evaluating one's willingness to work at the edge of competence are the starting points for moving out of one's comfort zone onto the edge of competence. Children can learn a process that will have them systematically taking realistic risks as part of their learning.

Competency #3: SMART Goal Setting

Because we know that motivation and achievement are affected by goal setting, isn't it surprising that most of us do little more than give it lip service? Goals affect performance and motivation in three ways. They:

- focus attention,
- influence persistence, and
- energize people.

More difficult goals tend to increase persistence, provided that children have some control over the amount of time they have available to work. More challenging goals tend to lead to higher performance than less challenging goals. That's one of the reasons why it's very important to keep your expectations high for your children.

Long-term goals must be broken down so that it's possible to attain goals fairly quickly and get regular feedback. Children need frequent feedback about their performance toward specific goals in order to adjust their effort or strategy. Without feedback, they have no way of knowing how they are doing.

Goals are most effective when they're challenging but attainable. Goals that are not accepted by your children probably will not influence their performance positively and may influence it negatively. In some cases, simply assigning a challenging goal can raise a child's belief in his abilities because it communicates a confidence that he has the ability to accomplish the task.

The acronym SMART stands for *specific, measurable, attainable, realistic,* and *timely.* In Chapter 4, we'll see how you can use it on a daily basis to focus your children on their highest priorities. When children feel excited and empowered to take charge of their learning and their lives, they become much more engaged in the learning process.

Competency #4: Mental Rehearsal

Terry Orlick, a well-known sports psychologist, says that when your performance falls apart, it usually falls apart in your head first. Mental rehearsal means to practice in your mind. Research on mental rehearsal draws three strong conclusions:

- mental rehearsal is better than no practice at all,
- mental rehearsal in combination with physical practice is more effective than either in isolation, and
- mental rehearsal enhances confidence and self-control more than motor tasks.

How many children do you know who would achieve more if they had strong beliefs in themselves and their abilities?

Given the strength of the research findings regarding the benefits of mental rehearsal in some domains, it's surprising that this skill is not promoted more. The potential benefits for relatively simple, but high-stakes performance tasks such as standardized tests, auditions, or competitions, are obvious.

Mental rehearsal also can help with relatively simple but challenging tasks, like giving an oral presentation or having a difficult conversation. The ability to visualize a desired performance in one's head improves performance.

Competency #5: Optimism

Why do some talented people persevere through challenges while others give up easily? A key factor is their explanatory style, or how they explain their success and failure. Children who blame themselves for their losses, who catastrophize setbacks, and who think that the causes of disappointments will last forever achieve much less than children who attribute losses to external factors, who limit the effects of setbacks, and who view a disappointment as a challenge to be conquered.

Researchers agree that explanatory style can be shaped. It's possible to become more optimistic, to learn to bounce back more easily after experiences of failure. To build optimism in our children, we must understand its three dimensions, evaluate our children's explanatory styles, and use language and exercises that coach kids toward greater optimism.

We begin by introducing the concepts of optimism and pessimism and raising children's awareness that, just as they have personal preferences for clothing, music, and hair, they also have style preferences for how they think about circumstances in their lives. We teach them how to shape that style with feedback, questions, and activities that provide practice with greater optimism and hope. We show them how to play detective and search for evidence that supports their conclusions or proves them wrong, so that they learn to be more accurate in their perspectives. Most importantly, we evaluate our own explanatory style and adapt our feedback to children so that our comments influence them to think positively about their success and failure experiences.

Competency #6: Mood Management

Did you know that emotions are some of the best predictors of achievement? Mood directly impacts our attention and our ability to control our minds. It shapes our thoughts and our focus. Consistent performance at high levels requires the ability to keep arousal within an optimal zone of functioning for the task.

Elite performers understand their mood very well. They master strategies that enable them to efficiently enter and exit their best mood states in order to give an outstanding performance every time. They typically stick to a strict daily regimen of diet, practice, exercise, rest, and self-talk in order to keep themselves in this zone of optimal functioning. They can't afford not to.

The role of mood management in achievement has been especially well investigated among athletes and creative achievers. Studies find that people who are consistently highly productive over the long term generally are people who keep themselves free from troubling mood states. They keep themselves in the zone—the zone of optimal functioning.

There is almost as wide of a range of tools for mood management as there are individuals. In minutes you can pass along to your children simple strategies that will help keep them in the mood for work. You can raise your children's awareness of their own mood patterns and how they relate to their achievement. You can teach them strategies that will maintain their energy and manage their zeal. You can demonstrate simple steps that will sharpen their focus and extend their concentration. You can coach them through small steps that eventually lead to big achievement.

Competency #7:
An Ability to Resolve the Need to Belong With the Need to Achieve

Conflicts often arise in talented children when their achievement values are not shared by mainstream culture. When this happens, children struggle to reconcile conflicting messages about what goals to pursue. For instance, smart girls hear messages like:

- Be smart, but don't be too smart.
- Compete, but be nice.
- Achieve, but take care of others too.

Talented youth from some racial or ethnic backgrounds might hear:

- Do well, but don't draw attention to yourself.
- Achieve, but don't act White.
- Get a good education, but don't leave the area.

And, in Western cultures, kids from humble or working-class backgrounds sometimes hear:

- Why do you have to go to college?
- You think you're better than we are?
- A paycheck is more important than school.

Unless children are able to recognize these conflicts for what they are—societal phenomena—and unless they have strategies for resolving the tensions that arise when they encounter them, there's a danger that they will stop striving for greater achievement.

We know that many talented youth need pointed assistance in negotiating two or more cultures simultaneously and we know that there are supports and interventions that help.

Children need to explore issues of identity and achievement, and to listen to achievers older than they are talk about the psychological costs of success. They need cultural brokers—adults who understand gender, class, or racial cultures well enough to explain cultural symbols in a variety of contexts, to talk them through potential conflicts, and to build bridges across contexts. And, they need direct instruction in the social skills required to negotiate a variety of contexts.

Conditioning is the foundation from which dreams are built. It provides the necessary grounding. It includes practice in the skills of the discipline, as well as practice in the psychological skills associated with a great performance. As one's level of achievement rises, so do the psychological demands associated with it.

Children must be psychologically prepared to deal with the mental and emotional demands of hard work and high performance. You can teach them. Each of us has limitations, yes, but these can be extended.

Studies across the domains of business, athletics, education, and the arts suggest that realizing the promise of high potential takes more than talent and hard work. It requires seven habits that can be nurtured. By putting in place the psychological factors that mediate motivation, effort, and initiative, you can see a significant increase in your child's achievement.

The difference between a good performance and a great performance often is mental. The highest levels of performance are reached when talented individuals have the basic psychological skills necessary to keep moving along the trajectory of achievement. You can involve yourself in helping your child discover the mental patterns associated with his or her best and less than best performance.

Practicing the exercises and strategies described in the following pages will help your children change from people whose nerves interfere with their achievement to those who are confident they can give their best performance. From children who become discouraged and retreat in the face of adversity, to children who sustain an effort over time. From children who go through the motions of schooling, to children with a focus and an aim. From children whose performance varies greatly from one week to the next, to children who consistently achieve.

Many young people don't develop their talent because they have no one to help them learn these skills. At the highest levels of accomplishment, success is more of a mental game than anything else and the best instructors know that this game can be taught. We shouldn't wait until children reach the highest levels of achievement to begin teaching them, however, or many young people will quit before they get there. We should be forming these habits along the way. I hope this book helps you and your child do just that.

Learning to Tolerate Stress and Anxiety

That was the toughest challenge, keeping the stress from rising up and taking over.

—Tara VanDerveer, Coach of the 1996 U.S. Olympic women's basketball team

NERVOUSNESS is a natural part of performance. We should expect it. Some people feel nervous when they are about to speak in front of a group. Others experience it when they're facing deadlines or being evaluated. Most people experience a lot of nervousness when the stakes are high. It's OK to be nervous, but you don't want to lose your nerve. If you don't have confidence that you can keep a lid on your anxiety, you will shy away from things that make you nervous. You'll avoid or procrastinate. You'll say no to opportunities you should accept. You'll turn away from challenges you should pursue.

Sound familiar? Britta, in the illustration below, is a good example.

DOI: 10.4324/9781003237068-2

REAL LIFE

Britta already is an experienced pianist at the age of 14. She's been playing for 10 years and performing for 3. Although she is highly skilled, she is having trouble giving her best at competitions because, as she puts it,

The pressure gets to me. I start getting nervous days before the event. Often I feel sick, and then I just want it to be over. On the day of the competition I can't eat and I'm all worked up about it. I start thinking I'm terrible and worry that I'll make a fool of myself. That never happens, but it doesn't matter, I worry just the same every time I have an important competition. I can make myself sick with the worry and stress. I love piano. I used to think that I wanted to be a professional musician, but I don't know any more. I don't think I can handle the stress. I hate this part of it.

Britta's experience is not uncommon. Many people aspire to do great things and then find themselves unable to tolerate the pressures that come with working at top levels. They wonder, "How long can I keep this up?" The increased stress slowly erodes the pleasures they enjoyed from their achievements and eats away at their confidence. After a while, burdened with so much stress and anxiety, they begin to ask themselves, "Is it worth it?"

As children move from one level of achievement to the next, their level of stress or anxiety goes up. As competition intensifies and stakes rise, so does that nervous, fearful feeling that they're not going to do well. Some children are more vulnerable to stress than others, but one thing is universal—developing talent requires a tolerance for stress and anxiety. We don't improve without it.

We need stress. Stress is good for us. Stress gets such a bad rap that we sometimes forget that it has its upside. Stress is not the enemy—it keeps us alert, keeps us motivated, and makes life interesting. Stress keeps us working hard. It only causes trouble when we don't know how to keep it under control or how to make it work for us. A key to high performance is understanding our personal stress patterns and learning to use tools that make those patterns work *for us* rather than *against us*. The overall goal is to keep stress at levels that optimize our performance.

Managing anxiety is the first step in the inner game of high achievement. To begin, use short sentence completions like the ones in the What Makes You Nervous? worksheet on p. 16 to help your children identify those things that contribute to their stress or anxiety. The repeated phrases help children carefully consider what makes them nervous.

You can teach your children simple tools for making the most of their stress. Because these tools are straightforward and easy to use, it's no problem to incorporate them into the day-to-day activities of your home. Make these habits part of the daily routine. Without them, your children will not develop their talent to its fullest potential. Mastering these tools is simple to do and with practice your children can get very good at it. At its simplest, learning to manage anxiety means learning to:

- breathe,
- relax, and
- keep moving toward the things that scare you.

When practiced regularly, these three strategies are extremely effective in keeping anxiety under control. Here's how you teach them.

Learning to Breathe

The most basic stress management skill is breathing. Breath is especially effective at keeping anxiety from spiraling out of control, and in maintaining concentration and focus. It keeps a lid on anxi-

What Makes You Nervous?

I feel nervous when I _____

_____.

I get apprehensive about _____

_____.

I worry about _____

_____.

_____

_____scares me.

I am most tense when_____

_____.

_____

_____ makes me anxious.

I feel stressed out when_____

_____.

I am afraid of _____

_____.

_____

_____puts me on edge.

I also feel nervous when _____

_____.

ety. Fear creates tension and breathing fights this tension by keeping oxygen levels high in the bloodstream.

The best breath technique is called *controlled* or *diaphragmatic breathing*, and it's most effective when sustained for several minutes. Children who master controlled breathing (sometimes called belly breathing) will feel more in control when they're nervous. Here's how you teach it. With children seated in a chair, give the following directions as you model where your children can see you.

Say, "Place one hand beneath your belly button and the other on your chest, keeping your chest up. If you collapse when you sit, you won't be able to breathe properly. Breathe normally for about 15 seconds, paying attention to your hands."

After about 15 seconds, ask your children to tell you which hand moves more. Then tell them that both hands may move, but if they're relaxed and breathing properly, the hand on their abdomen should move more than the hand on their chest. The hand on their chest will move some as their lungs fill and empty with air, but their lower hand should be moving up and down if their diaphragm is doing the work of breathing.

Tell them to leave their hands on their chest and abdomen and concentrate on breathing so that their lower hand rises and falls noticeably. Their belly should *move out when they breathe in* because the diaphragm is opening the chest cavity, and their belly should *move in when they exhale* because the diaphragm is tightening and squeezing the air out of their lungs. They don't need to push or pull their abdomen in or out. They should just let it happen naturally and notice the movement.

Do they feel the action of their diaphragm? That's the kind of breathing they need to do to control their anxiety. Controlled, or diaphragmatic, breathing is the key to managing stress when we're nervous.

Your children may need a minute or two to get the hang of this. If they're young, suggest they lie on the floor and put a book on their belly to see it rise and fall. If they're older, you can suggest they exaggerate the action to raise their awareness. They might see how far out they can push their bottom hand, or what it feels like to breathe mostly through their chest. Once they have experienced the differences between shallow and deep breathing, share with them that this is an excellent tool to use when they are feeling nervous. Breathing won't make all nervous feelings go away, but it will help them to stay calmer. Breath keeps a lid on nervous feelings.

As you continue to coach them over the next few weeks, continue to emphasize that slow breathing works best when we keep at it for several minutes. Use a timer initially to help them understand what it feels like to breathe for that long.

Practical Help

Some children are more motivated to use a new skill when they understand how it works. If that's true for your children, here's a more detailed explanation of what happens when we use controlled breathing.

When we're very nervous our muscles tighten, even our diaphragm muscles. As a result, we tend to breathe more through our upper chest. This is why it's sometimes hard to get our breath when we're afraid. Our muscles are tight. Breathing through our upper chest is called *shallow breathing*—it's what all of us tend to do when we're tense.

When our breathing is shallow, we don't get enough oxygen into our bloodstream. As our oxygen levels drop, we start to feel lightheaded or dizzy, weak-kneed and unsteady; we may have sweaty palms, or our heart pounds, or we may feel sick to our stomach. These are the result of not getting enough oxygen.

Often, these symptoms make our nervousness worse because we start to pay attention to how we're feeling and worry that we won't perform well. This spiral of nerves can lead in some cases to a full-blown panic attack. All of us can relate to the experience of spiraling anxiety. It's not fun!

Breathing in a controlled fashion *for 4 minutes* restores the oxygen levels in our blood stream. As the body gets enough oxygen, muscles relax and we start to feel more in control and less nervous.

Together with your child, set a timer for 4 minutes and breathe together silently, with hands on your chest and abdomen, until the timer rings. Most people are surprised at how long 4 minutes is.

Without practice, most people don't know to pay attention to the rise and fall of their abdomen and they don't realize they should keep it up for 4 minutes. This little exercise teaches children the basics they need to know to begin to use their breath to control their anxiety.

Once your children understand the difference between shallow and controlled breathing, help them work toward mastery of this technique by taking a couple of very short breathing breaks every day for a week. Doing so communicates that this is an important skill to learn and that they need to practice to master it. Take advantage of those short breaks when you're waiting in line or in the car, and during transitions from school to home. You can say something like, "Let's take a short breathing break," and model for them. Remember to breathe deeply and slowly from your diaphragm and place your hand below your belly button if it helps you to focus. It's important to keep your shoulders back so that your lungs can expand fully.

Perhaps your children know quite a bit about breath control because they've seen a speech therapist, have medical conditions that affect their lungs, or take yoga or singing lessons. If so, ask them to teach you! Until mid-adolescence, children are eager to share what they know with their parents. Speech therapists and vocal or instrumental music teachers know a lot about breath control. If you have access to one, ask him or her to show you some additional techniques.

Continue to prompt your kids (and yourself!) to use what you've taught them every day for another 2 weeks to help them develop the habit of paying attention to their breath and their anxiety. For instance, before any potential anxiety-provoking situation—a test, a presentation, a match, etc.—put your hand on your abdomen and say, "Remember to breathe. It will help you feel in control." During moments when they must maintain a sharp focus or concentration say, "Remember your breath." Bring up the topic of managing anxiety and using breath to control fear in your casual conversations.

Adopt the attitude of an adventurer, a scientist, or psychologist and conduct experiments with your kids over the following weeks. Suggest that every child apply the 4-minute breath technique sometime during the week when he or she is especially nervous or stressed and then take a few minutes when you're together to report on its effectiveness. Did your children notice a difference in how they felt? Were they able to be nervous without losing their nerve? What effect did the breathing have on their confidence? On their focus or concentration? If you're homeschooling or have opportunities to work this into your children's schoolwork, you could use the worksheet I've provided on p. 22 to write up the results of your experiment. Note that the title is deliberately scientific sounding, as it lends an air of importance to the endeavor. The important thing is to have fun while you practice the technique until your child has mastered it.

Once you believe your kids have mastered the technique, use what you've learned. When you see them getting anxious, or you know they're going to be dealing with a situation that tends to make them nervous, cue them to use their breath control. Use one liners or a gesture (patting your belly button might be useful) to remind them to breathe diaphragmatically. When they're struggling with feelings of frustration, when they seem to be losing their patience, when they're becoming distracted by nerves, in any situation that appears to escalate their anxiety, cue them to breathe. Remind them from time to time that if they're already nervous, it will take 4 minutes before they feel like they have a lid on their anxiety. Keep practicing.

If one or more of your children have an especially hard time with shyness, worries, or a specific fear, encourage them to keep practicing their controlled breathing until they feel confident that they are improving their ability to manage their stress. Some of us are more prone to anxiety than others, and sometimes life circumstances give birth to fear for a season of time. Because kids take their cues from their parents, you can be a big help to your children in their efforts to manage stress if you model confidence in their ability to master these strategies and encourage them to keep using what they've learned. At times like these, parents find it often helps to say something that validates their children's struggle while also encouraging their effort. Here are some suggestions:

- I know this is hard. Use what you've learned.
- I can see that this is tough for you. I'm confident you'll learn how to handle this.
- I wish I could make it better. Remember to use your breath.
- This is a big challenge. I know you'll get it eventually.

Once your child has mastered learning to breathe, the next step is learning to relax.

Effects of Controlled Breathing on Perceptions of Self-Control Trial # ___

Date of Experiment: _____

Procedure: (Describe what you did.)

_____
_____
_____
_____
_____

Observations: (What did you notice?)

_____
_____
_____
_____
_____

Results: (What happened?)

_____
_____
_____
_____
_____

WORKSHEET

Learning to Relax

It's impossible to be relaxed and afraid at the same time. Fear produces tension, while relaxation releases that tension. Relaxation is not optional for high achievement. It's essential. This is why people who want to improve their ability to manage stress learn to relax. Serious high achievers get really good at it.

Maybe your children think they don't have time to relax. Perhaps they feel they don't have the time to complete the things they have to do now, and maybe you feel this way too. Many of us tend to admire people who are under a lot of strain yet still try to accomplish things.

High-achieving children sometimes confuse emotional and physical intensity. They think that if they aren't feeling distressed, they aren't working hard enough. Parents may confuse this too. Passionate expression and intense power do not come from *pressuring* the body and mind, however, but from *releasing* the body and mind to work together easily and efficiently. Focused relaxation concentrates abilities, resulting in a better outcome with less stress. Every great athlete knows that recovery and renewal are essential for sustaining high performance. Elite performers in the arts and business know it too.

Relaxing doesn't mean not working hard. It means working hard without tension. People who can relax are efficient. They get the same results or better with less effort. As your children relax, their minds will calm and focus. The better they are at releasing unwanted tension, the more your children will be able to perform to the best of their abilities.

Learning to relax involves controlled breathing and recognizing the difference between tension and relaxation in your body. When you can recognize tension that is detrimental to your performance, you can reduce it with a variety of strategies. One highly effective technique is called *progressive muscle relaxation.*

Progressive muscle relaxation does just what it says. It relaxes one group of muscles after another in steps or stages. Children alternately tense and relax major muscle groups, working top down or bottom up, for a full 5 seconds of tension, followed by 10–15 seconds of relaxation. Major muscle groups include the forehead, eyes, jaws, neck, shoulders, upper back, biceps, forearms, hands, abdomen, groin, legs, hips, thighs, buttocks, calves, and feet.

It's very important when you teach this to follow the directions exactly the first few times. Novices commonly make two mistakes: They skip some major muscle groups, and they try to shorten the exercise too soon. The problem with this is that even as a parent, you don't know in what part of their bodies your children carry most of their tension. Most people carry their stress in a particular area; some people clench their jaw, for instance, while others tighten their neck and shoulders. Many people carry their stress in their lower back. If you skip a major muscle group, your children could do the entire exercise without ever relaxing that part of their body where they carry most of their stress. They need to do all of the major muscle groups initially to learn how and where they carry their tension.

Learning to relax takes practice. No one learns it in a day. And, once we learn to relax, we have to continue practicing until it becomes a habit. People need to practice progressive relaxation daily for at least 2 weeks to approach mastery. After that, you can begin to abbreviate the exercise by eliminating some muscle groups. However, it's important to emphasize the muscle groups that tend to give your children trouble.

The worksheet on pp. 26–28 includes a script to get you started with progressive relaxation. Read aloud to yourself the script once through using a timer, so that you have a feel for the pacing, and then, when you're ready to do it with your children, read it aloud very slowly. It should take you about 12–15 minutes. If you'd like to do the exercise together with your children, try tape-recording the script and playing it back for all of you to hear. Or, alternatively, you can go to any of several Web sites to click on audio files that will play a soothing version you can use together. Here are a couple you might try:

- http://www.hws.edu/studentlife/resources/counseling/relax.asp
- http://www.healingbridge.com/progrelaxaudio.htm

Note that in the script, each part of the body is bolded in order to ensure that you hit all of the major areas that need relaxation. Also, specific points for pause are included in parentheses.

Just like learning to play a game or instrument, practicing the technique over and over will develop your children's skill and increase their confidence. Ideally, the goal is to reach the point that they are so aware of the differences between a relaxed and a tense body that they can relax their body with a simple verbal cue like *relax* or *let go*.

REAL LIFE

Sara Fisher, the youngest person to race in the Indianapolis 500 at age 19, had to learn to manage anxiety in order to succeed at what she loves: racecar driving. She says (Ungerleider, 2005):

In a race car, you're wedged tight into that cockpit and you'll be there for 500 miles going almost 200 miles an hour or more for at least two and a half hours. You're under a lot of pressure, both mentally and physically. Mentally, there's the fact that when you're in that car, you have to pay attention to every minute. In this sport, a tiny mistake can send you spinning into the wall at 200 mph or crashing into someone else at that speed and wrecking a quarter of a million dollar car.

Practical Help:
Script for Progressive Relaxation

You can sit in your chair or lay on the floor if you like. Get comfortable where you are. Drop your shoulders; loosen your neck and your legs. You may want to close your eyes. Take a few slow, deep breaths (pause). Inhale and exhale slowly. It doesn't matter if you breathe through your nose or your mouth, but it helps to keep your inhalations and exhalations about the same length.

Now, grip your **fists** as tight as you can. Hold them shut and notice the pressure in your forearms. Now let go. Feel the tension flow away from your arm and fingers, and notice the relaxation. Do it again. Clench your **fists** (pause). Hold them shut, and now let go. Notice the difference between tension and relaxation. Do it one more time on your own.

Now bend your **arms** at the elbows and press your arms against your body as tightly as you can. Squeeze your biceps (pause) and hold, noticing the pressure you feel. Now let go. Feel the tension drain from your arms. Repeat it one more time—bend your elbows, squeeze your arms, and hold them tightly (pause). Then, relax (pause).

Scrunch up your **forehead** as tightly as you can. And, relax (pause). Smooth out your forehead as much as you can, letting the energy drain down your face. Now, frown and feel the strain across your **face.** Frown as hard as you can. Now let go (pause). Feel the relaxation spread around your forehead, mouth, and chin. Close your **eyes,** and squeeze them tightly. Pay attention to the tension you feel. Keep your eyes closed, and let them relax (pause). Keep them comfortably and gently closed.

Now, clench your **jaw.** Bite hard (pause). Notice how it feels (pause). Now let go. Feel your lips part slightly as your mouth and jaw fully relax (pause). Press your **tongue** against the roof of your mouth. Push. Feel the strain on your tongue (pause). Relax (pause). Purse your lips, pressing them forward as tight as you can (pause). Now let go. Feel the tension draining from your forehead, eyes, jaw, and tongue.

Roll your head comfortably back and notice where the tension lies (pause). Now, roll it to the left (pause), then roll it gently to the right. Bring your head slowly forward and rest your chin on your chest. Pay attention to the tension in the back of your **neck.** Focus on it. Now continue to breathe deeply, letting your head return to a comfortable position (pause). Lift your **shoulders**. Try to touch your ears with the tops of your shoulders. Really stretch. Press and hold (pause). Now let your shoulders go completely and be aware of the tension release. Feel the release through your shoulders, neck, and arms. Drop your shoulders some more. You should feel more and more relaxed.

Give your whole body a chance to relax. Notice the heaviness of your body. Let your weight sink into the chair (or floor). Take a deep breath and hold it (pause). Now exhale, and feel your chest loosen. Let all of the air escape. Do this again, widening your rib cage and holding your breath, then easily releasing all of the air. Repeat one more time (pause). Notice the tension draining from your body.

Now, place one hand on your **abdomen**, tighten your stomach, and hold (pause). Relax (pause). Keeping your hand on your stomach, push your hand up with your abdominal muscles and hold (pause). Now let go. Notice the difference. Now, arch your **back** without straining. Focus the tension in your lower back, tightening. Let go, and relax deeper and deeper (pause).

Tighten your **hips and thighs**. Press your heels down as hard as you can into the floor and hold the tension (pause). Now relax. Curl your toes tightly. Feel the grip in your **feet, ankles,** and **lower calves** (pause). Let go, and feel the energy moving in your feet. Now curl your toes up, toward the ceiling, and hold (pause). Relax again.

As you relax, notice that your body feels heavier and heavier. Feel the relaxation spread deeply through your calves, thighs, abdomen, back, arms, shoulders, and head. Let go some more (pause). Notice the feeling of looseness throughout your body (pause). I will count backward from five and as I do, shift your attention from your body to your surroundings. Five, four, three . . . notice the presence of others around you, the sounds outside . . . two, one . . . open your eyes feeling refreshed and energized.

Ping-Pong Breath

It's easiest to do ping-pong breath lying on your back, but you can do it at your desk, too, or even while standing. Try it first when lying on your back. Imagine that a ping-pong ball sits on your lips. It's very light. Now, imagine yourself blowing that ping-pong ball up into the air, high above your head. Blow out as long as you can, seeing that ball rise until you can make it rise no farther. Then, inhale slowly, descending the ball in your mind. Keep the ball traveling downward on your gentle stream of air. When the ball reaches your lips, exhale again, pushing the ball slowly into the air as high as you can. Repeat for at least 4 minutes.

Some children who have trouble falling asleep find that doing this exercise for 10 minutes when they first turn off the lights clears their mind and helps them to relax enough to sleep.

REAL LIFE

Eduardo has trouble falling asleep at night. "I can't stop thinking," he says. "My brain keeps thinking and I can't make it stop. I go to bed and lay in the dark and think."

Eduardo's father taught him how to use progressive relaxation to calm his mind. He and Eduardo made their own recording and Eduardo listens to it at bedtime with some background music that he finds especially soothing. "The music and the words make my mind slow down so I can fall asleep," he says.

When he's not able to use the tape, or he's having trouble focusing his attention, Eduardo tries another exercise he likes called *ping-pong breath*.

While you're practicing these exercises with your kids over the coming weeks, use these questions to get your children talking about when and where they might use these tools:

- When was the last time you felt nervous? Where were you and what was happening?
- If you were confident you could manage your fear, what would you try that you haven't done?

- Some people have said that courage is to feel afraid and act any-way. What do you think? Are you brave if you're not afraid?

Once your children have mastered controlled breathing and learning to relax, they have only one more thing to learn to be competent in managing their anxiety: They have to keep moving toward the things that scare them.

Action Is the Antidote for Fear

Jaya is a quiet 17-year-old with strong math skills. She's in an accelerated math track at her school and plans to go to the university to earn an engineering degree. She is known as a shy girl who works hard. What most of her classmates don't know, however, is that Jaya is not just shy, she's afraid.

She's afraid to open her mouth in class for fear that someone will laugh. She's afraid to tell a joke she heard because she thinks every-one will think she's stupid. She's afraid to speak to her classmates in the halls because she fears they will humiliate her. Jaya clams up in class because it frightens her to speak in front of others. She keeps to herself and does her work quietly.

This year Jaya is taking a number of advanced classes in hopes of strengthening her transcript for university applications. She's horrified to learn that in one of them she'll be expected to make a number of class presentations. The thought of speaking in front of her classmates makes her so anxious that Jaya is seriously considering dropping the class. Her counselor tells her, though, that dropping the class will make her less competitive for the university she wants to attend. Jaya is afraid of what will happen if she drops the class, and she fears what will happen if she stays in it. She's miserable.

Jaya's problem is not an uncommon one and fortunately, it's one that's easy to solve. She can stay in the class and learn to reduce her stress. In fact, she will need to learn to manage this fear if she wants to succeed because an inability to speak up in front of others will seriously compromise her future achievement.

There are three things people must practice in order to become skilled at managing their anxiety. We've already gone over two of them: learning to breathe and learning to relax. The third thing is to keep moving toward our fears. We must keep children moving toward the things that scare them.

Naturally, we want to either fight or flee when we feel overwhelmed by stress, but that only leads to more fighting and fleeing. To achieve our goals, we have to learn not to flee, but to keep moving toward things that make us nervous. We can teach these principles and provide children with tools that will help them take action. The less they resist, the more freedom of movement they have and the more efficient they are with their efforts. Try this little exercise to see what I mean.

Put one index finger into the fist of your other hand.

Now try to pull your index finger away from your clenched fist.

What happens?

Now try it again, but this time, try pushing your finger into your fist before you pull.

What happens now?

The more you pull, the more your fist holds on. When you move into the resistance, the tension is released and you can then pull your finger out easily.

It's human nature to stay away from things that scare us, but avoidance keeps fear going. That's the nature of fear. Children can learn to breathe and relax; they can tell themselves all kinds of positive messages, but if they continue to avoid the things that make them nervous, they will continue to have trouble managing their fear. The truth is that anxiety *grows bigger* the longer you stay away from it.

Jaya needs to determine one small step she could take in the direction of the thing she's resisting, such as saying hello to a classmate every day or raising her hand to offer an answer or idea once a day. Then, she must decide if she is willing to try it to see what happens.

To keep your kids moving in the direction of the things that scare them, begin by talking with them about the nature of anxiety. Knowledge is power, and when children understand the nature of anxiety, they are empowered to work with it rather than against it. Children who understand how anxiety operates have the information they need to strategically manage it.

I like to tell kids that anxiety is just like cold water. I ask them to imagine that it's an unusually hot day early in the summer season. It's so hot that your friends call to invite you to go swimming at the local pool or beach. Your first thought is, "Yeah! Let's go swimming!" But, then you hesitate because you remember that as early as it is in the season, the water is likely to be very cold. The pool won't be very heated yet. The water at the pool hasn't had time to warm up.

You have an approach/avoidance conflict. You want to go swimming, but you don't want to be uncomfortable in the cold water. So, you say yes to the invitation, but you don't promise that you'll get in.

Once at the beach or the pool, you lay in the sun, getting hotter and hotter. Eventually, you're so miserable that you can't stand it any longer and you decide to try out the water.

Now, people who get into the water get in one of two ways. Some people are run and jumpers. Are you in this category? At the pool, run and jumpers enter the water by climbing up the ladder of the diving board and running off the end. They don't stroll off the board; they run. At the lake or ocean, run and jumpers go to the end of the beach, often joining hands with their friends, and run as fast as they can to the water's edge, throwing themselves into the water.

Others, though, are toe-by-toe people. They get in ever so gradually. Perhaps this is more like you. Toe-by-toe people go to the shallow end and step into the water. They suck in their breath and their bellies and complain (often loudly!) about how cold the water is. They pace back and forth in ankle-deep water and whine and whimper. As they do this, what happens?

Their body is getting used to it! Exposure to a little bit of the cold water acclimates their feet and ankles so they're able to wander into even deeper water.

Toe-by-toe people then take a big breath and move to knee-deep water. They may continue to complain about how cold the water is until, within a minute or so, they're used to it again.

Unlike the run and jumpers who get used to the water temperature very quickly, toe-by-toe people move slowly into deeper and deeper water, giving themselves time at each new depth to get used to the temperature. Eventually, they reach waist-deep water and they have to decide whether they're in or they're out.

If they decide that the water is just too cold for swimming, they get out and may not go back into the water again for weeks, but if they decide to take the plunge, they immerse themselves by either diving under the water or bobbing completely under. And, they stay under until they're used to it.

We know from experience that our bodies acclimate fairly quickly once exposed. Once under the water, we all swim around until we're out of breath, allowing our bodies to adjust to the change in temperature. When we come up for air, we keep our chins at the surface of the water so we'll get used to the cold water faster. It doesn't take long before we feel comfortable and we're able to enjoy our time in the water.

Anxiety is just like that.

The wonderful thing about anxiety is that regardless of whether you run and jump or go toe-by-toe, if you expose yourself to an amount you can tolerate and keep yourself exposed, you'll get used to it. Your anxiety will go away, just as cold water feels warmer the longer you're exposed to it.

I love that about anxiety. It's uncomfortable, but it's a lot easier to learn to manage than anger or depression.

Once we've learned to breathe and can keep a lid on our anxiety, and to relax and release tension, the third step in learning to manage anxiety is to expose ourselves to what scares us and to keep ourselves in it until our nervousness decreases. Like toe-by-toe people, we can expose ourselves to our fears a little bit at a time, or we can immerse ourselves all at once like the run and jumpers. Sound simple? It is. All of us have had experiences we can relate to this phenomenon.

Many of us who get very nervous right before speaking in front of others will still say yes to public speaking because we know from experience that our fear will abate once we get started. Athletes who feel really anxious before competition look forward to the start of it because they know that once they get moving their nervousness will disappear. Musicians who feel apprehensive before a performance often wish it would begin, because they know from experience that once they begin to play or sing they'll start to feel better. Anxiety decreases when we take steps toward the things that scare us.

Moving *toward* the things that scare us is known as *exposure*. Just like acclimating to cold water, we must expose ourselves to the things that make us nervous in order to become comfortable with them. This does not have to be as scary as it may sound. We can move toward our fears in small steps.

Meili, for instance, feels anxious in all kinds of social situations. She noticed that it got much worse when she started middle school and had to change classes every hour. The lunchroom and hallways are where she feels the most nervous, so she takes her lunch to a teacher's room and eats with a couple of friends. She moves through the hallways as quickly as possible. She's not doing as well academically as she used to because she is reluctant to participate like she did in elementary school. The less she participates, the more nervous she gets about opening her mouth. Remember? Our fears grow when we avoid them. Worse yet, Meili feels lonely and left out at school because she is not a part of the social activities that go on during and between classes. She's not as connected as she was in grade school.

Meili's anxiety is not terribly specific. There are many circumstances that cause her to feel nervous. To help her figure out where to start, her counselor asks Meili to make a list of 10 situations in which she feels anxious, including the worst-case scenario. That's always the easiest to imagine.

After thinking about it, Meili came up with a list of 10 uncomfortable situations and ranked them in order from the most to the least anxiety-provoking. Here's her list:

10. Talking in front of the whole class.
9. Talking in front of a group of people I don't know.
8. Talking for a few minutes in a small group of people.
7. Speaking up at a student meeting when I don't agree.
6. Saying hello to a classmate in the hall.
5. Raising my hand to answer a question in class.
4. Eating lunch in the cafeteria.
3. Being called on by the teacher.

2. Imagining myself answering a question or speaking in class.

1. Watching a friend give a presentation in front of the class.

With her parents' and teacher's support, Meili begins by learning to control her breathing and relax her body. She practices for 3 weeks before applying them to the situations on her list. She moves toward her fear by starting with the easiest things at the bottom of her list first. She uses her breath and relaxation techniques to keep herself calm while watching classmates give short presentations in class, and she pays attention to her breath when she is called on by the teacher. Although she still feels nervous when she walks the hallway, by concentrating on her breathing and keeping her body relaxed, Meili notices that she can hang out in the hallway longer and talk with friends. The more she exposes herself to this situation while relaxed, the easier it becomes.

Eventually, by practicing her breath and relaxation techniques while deliberately putting herself in situations she used to avoid, Meili discovers that she can do many of the things on her list more easily than she thought. Buoyed up by pride in her courage and success, she slowly works toward the scarier things on her list until she is talking a lot more often than she once did. She still feels nervous in some large social situations, but she's a lot less avoidant of them. A presentation to the class makes her nervous, but she's confident that she can handle her nerves.

Summary

Elite performers learn how to tolerate stress and anxiety. They have to. They can't give their best day after day in stressful situations without having mastered tools for releasing tension. Learning to manage anxiety and to make their stress work for them, rather than against them, is fundamental to high achievement.

People who strive to excel learn to pay attention to their breath. They learn to relax and they expose themselves to the things that scare them. Learning to tolerate stress and anxiety is not complicated. It just takes practice. Learning to breathe, to relax, and to keep moving toward the things that scare them are three simple and effective tools for controlling stress and anxiety that children of any age can master.

Chapter Resources

Bourne, E., & Garano, L. (2003). *Coping with anxiety: 10 simple ways to relieve anxiety, fear & worry.* Oakland, CA: New Harbinger Publications.

Bruser, M. (1997). *The art of practicing: A guide to making music from the heart.* New York: Bell Tower.

Farhi, D. (1996). *The breathing book.* New York: Henry Holt & Co.

Merrel, K. (2001). *Helping children overcome depression and anxiety: A practical guide.* New York: Guilford Press.

Nichols, D. (1995, December). The demons within: Confronting performance anxiety. *Chamber Music Magazine*, 20–40.

—3—

Out of the Comfort Zone

Moving Your Children to Their Edge of Competence

Risks, I like to say, always pay off. You learn what to do or what not to do.

—Jonas Salk, M.D., developer of the polio vaccine

I have been a bit of a risk taker all my life.

—Sally Ride, first American woman in space

WE rise or fall to the level of those around us.

In some settings, people expect a lot from one another, spur one another on, and stimulate one another's efforts. In other settings, people expect little from one another, hold each other back, and even undermine the efforts of some. That's why people who are serious about success seek others with similar aspirations. They work or train with people who are at least as talented as they are, and even better. Working with others with more talent improves our own performance.

Your child will be more likely to continue on his trajectory of high achievement if he's part of a group that stimulates him to

 DOI: 10.4324/9781003237068-3

work harder. If he spends a lot of time with others whose expectations for effort or achievement are not as high, or who dismiss his goals or interests as unimportant, you can expect his performance to decline. Your goal is to have your child working with others who will make him better.

High achievement requires a willingness to work at the edge of one's competence. This is the place where results come with effort, and where your child has to reach. It's the place where tasks are challenging and where teammates or classmates have similar interests, abilities, and drive. It's a scary place, too, a place that requires risk.

Think about it. If your children can earn excellent grades and receive high praise during the first 6 or 7 years of school, without making much effort, what are all the things that they don't learn that other kids are learning?

• They don't learn how to study, because they don't have to.
• They don't learn how to manage their time.
• They don't learn to cope with disappointments and setbacks, or even failure.

If it doesn't take them long to get their work done and they can wait until the last minute, they don't develop good organizational skills. They might come to believe that the reason they're successful is because they're smart and that being smart means not having to make an effort. High school teachers will tell you that they have some kids who think they should get top grades just because they've showed up.

Your child's greatest accomplishments are achieved when he steps out of his comfort zone and reaches for challenging goals. Fifteen-year-old Troy, for instance, took a risk when he selected a difficult piece of music for his violin recital.

I knew that the music was too hard for me when I picked it but I really wanted to learn to play it because I thought the score was awesome. I had only 3 months to learn it, but the pressure motivated me to practice every day. Still, I couldn't play it without making mistakes. Parts of it were just too fast.

Three weeks before the recital I started to freak out because I still couldn't play some sections of it very well. I knew there was no way I was going to be able to play it the way I wanted, so I just practiced playing it through, mistakes and all. It helped that everyone was so supportive. My teachers knew the music was tough and my parents kept saying that the important thing was to give it a shot. The night of the recital, I played it better than I had ever played it at home, but I still made a lot of mistakes. It wasn't perfect but it was the best I had ever played and I got a standing ovation.

The Optimal Match

An appropriate level of challenge is essential for high achievement. It's what defines the edge of our competence and where the best learning takes place. If you want to learn play tennis, you don't sign up for an intermediate class. You look for a teacher and a class where you'll learn the fundamentals of the game. That's as much reach as you're ready for. But, if you're advanced and already play quite well, you look for a teacher who will provide you with the appropriate level of challenge based on your current skill level and readiness for new techniques. You play with people whose skill level and drive for the game matches your own. If you know someone whose backhand is weaker than yours but whose serve is much better, you know that playing with her will improve your ability to return a serve.

How do you know what's an appropriate level of reach for your children? It's the level where they are ready to learn something that they haven't mastered yet. They have *readiness,* but not *mastery.* This is sometimes called the *optimal match.*

All of us learn best when we have to reach and we have the scaffolding we need to help us make the grab. Sadly, in school, one of the things that sometimes happens to bright kids is that they have too little challenge. They spend a good deal of time on skills they've already mastered and don't get to move on to the skills they're now ready for. They aren't required to reach and are allowed to spend most of their time in their comfort zone. However, it also sometimes happens that certain kids have to reach too much, and don't have the support they need to succeed. I have an included an example from my own life that illustrates the difference in the box on the next page.

Your first step in moving your kids to their edge of competence is to make sure they're learning from teachers and coaches who make them reach.

The Importance of Risk

Does your child prefer to stay in her comfort zone instead of moving to her edge of competence? Sticking to the things she already knows how to do well feels secure, but it's not how growth happens. A critical step in empowering talented children to reach and realize their potential is to teach them the importance of working at their edge of competence and encouraging them to take the steps that keep them there.

REAL LIFE

When my husband and I were dating, we used to play racquetball together a couple of times a week. He was an exceptionally good player and I was just a beginner so I always lost by a lot, at least 11 points. Within a matter of minutes I'd be behind by 4 or 5 points, but I would hang on, fighting to keep every point. By the time the score was 10 to 2 or 12 to 3, however, I had little motivation or desire left for the game. Losing so badly discouraged me, and took a lot of fun out of the game. Beating me so easily did not make for an especially interesting game for my husband, either. One day we decided to handicap me 11 points to even out the challenge. What a change that made for us! Now every game started as a close game. He would have to press to catch up and keep me from gaining a point, and I worked very hard to earn the few points I needed to win before he evened the score. I was much more motivated because I perceived that the goal was within reach.

Handicapping me 11 points did not quite present enough of a challenge to my husband, however. One day, he beat me by only one point. I felt great! I had made great progress. My elation was dampened, however, when he told me that he had played the whole game with his left hand. He instinctively had looked for a way to increase the reach for himself.

What kind of risk taker is your child? How easy is it for her to take a chance on the things that are important to her? Sometimes, it's the most capable kids who are the most risk avoidant. They shrink from challenge because they're unsure of the outcomes. They're so used to being one of the best that they're unprepared to handle the emotions that arise when their performance falls short. They have little experience with disappointment, rejection, or setbacks. They don't handle criticism well, and they're not used to working hard. They don't want to be uncomfortable. They don't want to be distressed.

Sound like anybody you know?

Learning to take realistic risks increases our confidence about what we can do, and our sense of self-control. Risk taking also helps develop those strategies for managing anxieties and overcoming fears that we talked about in Chapter 2. It also provides practice in important decision making. Children often don't have the opportunity to make meaningful decisions, but the fun family exercise on the next page will enable you to give your children regular opportunities to make important decisions for their own lives.

Where Do You Start?

Start with yourself and ask the question: What am I modeling? Your example is the most effective teacher. As you read through the exercises that follow, consider them for yourself before you apply them to your children. Remember, your kids are watching.

Let's begin by defining risk. What does it mean to take a chance? Your kids will have their own responses, but many children say things like:

- Doing something I'm not sure will work out.
- Doing something where I might fail.
- Doing something scary.
- Doing something dangerous.

Talk with your children about whether they think it's possible to live a satisfying and rewarding life without taking some risks. If you discuss it with three or more children, I promise you a stimulating dialogue. As a follow up, try these questions:

- Do you think you can you live life without taking risks?
- Would you want to?
- What kind of life would that be?

Where's Your Edge of Competence?

In the **Comfort Zone** at the center of the bull's eye, list those things that you are very good at, those activities at which you always succeed.

In the **Confidence Zone**, list those things that you are confident you can do well some of the time.

At the **Edge of Competence**, list those things that you wish you could do well but still require a lot of effort.

In the **Out of Your League Zone**, list those things that you would like to do someday but that right now are truly out of your reach.

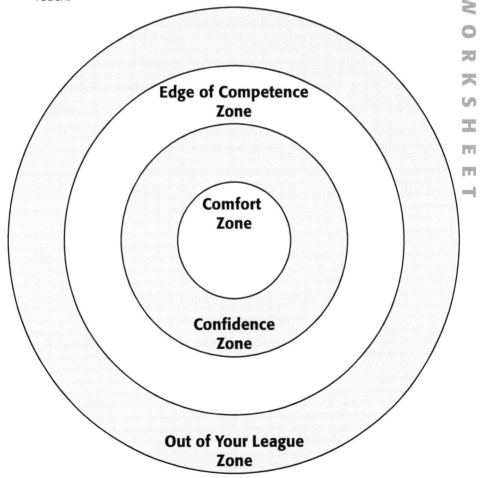

Peak Performance for Smart Kids • Copyright © Taylor & Francis Group This page may be photocopied or reproduced with permission for individual use.

The truth is that life is full of risk, whether we're aware of it or not. Driving is risky. So is falling in love, applying for a job, and having children. It's impossible to live life without taking chances. People who develop the habit of systematically taking risks have a lot more fun.

Invite your children to explore with you the ways in which realistic risk-taking relates to health, achievement, and satisfying relationships. Discuss the lives of people they admire. What kinds of risks do they see these people taking? Talk about leaders they know at school, in your community, and in the news. Is there a relationship between risk taking and leadership? What examples can they share? Use the activity on the Practical Help worksheet on page 47 to expand your children's understanding of the concept of risk and its relationship to achievement.

Occasionally, adolescents confuse thrill seeking with risk-taking. It's important to clarify the difference. Thrill seeking often is the product of boredom or a need to prove oneself. Unlike risk-taking, the only point of thrill seeking is the surge of excitement, the adrenaline rush. Consequently, it becomes necessary over time to seek greater thrills in order to continue the illusion of growth or change. Thrill seeking, unlike risk-taking, has no real substantive value. The risk-taking we're talking about here is realistic. It's purposeful, rational, and authentic:

- it's purposeful because its aim is to develop courage and persistence,
- it's rational because it is grounded in the needs, interests, and abilities of the individual, and
- it's authentic because it is personally relevant and meaningful.

Practical Help

1. Think of someone whose accomplishments you admire or respect. It can be anyone, past or present. It can be someone you know personally or someone who's famous. In one or two sentences describe what they have achieved that you admire.

_____

_____

_____

_____

2. Now consider what this person has risked in order to realize his or her achievement. Examine the chances he or she took socially, emotionally, physically, or intellectually, and list as many of them as you can. If the person is someone you know well, ask him or her to share one or two risks he or she took when he or she was your age that helped reach his or her goals.

_____

_____

_____

_____

3. Do you think this person could have accomplished what he or she did without taking some of these risks? Why or why not?

_____

_____

_____

_____

W O R K S H E E T

Becoming a Better Risk Taker

Risk-taking is inherently failure-prone. Otherwise it would be called sure-thing-taking.

—Financial commentator, Tim MacMahon

You can encourage your children to step out of their comfort zones and work at their edge of competence. You can teach them to be better risk takers. The first step is making them aware of their own patterns of risk-taking. Begin by sharing with them the five categories of risk. They are:

- intellectual,
- social,
- emotional,
- physical, and
- moral or spiritual.

Invite your children to share examples of risks in each category, adding a few of your own.

For instance, *intellectual risks* test the limits of your thinking power. When you take an intellectual risk, you're exploring how smart you really are, what your intellectual capacity is. Examples of intellectual risks for your child may include:

- trying the extra credit question,
- choosing to read a book that's harder than what he usually reads,
- enrolling in an advanced class, or
- answering a tough question.

For some kids, just raising their hand in class to answer a question is a risk, and for others, it's daring to try the next level of difficulty. Letting others know that you're smarter than them, or not as smart, also can be an intellectual risk.

Social risks involve situations with other people. They're often scary because you compare yourself to others and believe that you come up short. Social risks happen when you feel concerned about what others are going to think. One of the top three fears people have—public speaking—is a social risk. (The other two are physical—going to the dentist and flying.) Other social risks might include:

- talking to someone you don't know,
- going to a social event alone,
- speaking up when you disagree, or
- being friends with someone who's unpopular or controversial.

Emotional risk involves being honest with your feelings. Many people don't like emotional risks. It can be frightening to be authentic or real. Consider these challenges:

- letting someone in authority know that you're upset with a decision he or she made,
- acknowledging that you feel afraid or sad,
- expressing your anger toward someone, or
- caring deeply for someone.

How many of those would you be willing to do? How difficult do they seem? We tend to avoid situations that we fear may upset us or make us cry. We also fear other people's disapproval or rejection.

Physical risks are the easiest to imagine. Bungee jumping and skydiving always come to mind. But, for some kids, gym class is a physical risk (and for others it's a social risk because they're so concerned about what other kids are thinking about their appearance or performance.) For many young children, the playground equipment is an attractive challenge, but to others it is scary. They don't want to climb, spin, or be pushed on a swing. Physical risks also might involve:

- running a race,
- learning to ski,
- opening your eyes under water, or
- going to the doctor or dentist.

Finally, *moral* or *spiritual risks* have to do with our strongest convictions and our highest values. Taking a stand against an injustice, doing the right thing even though it's costly, or speaking up for something we believe in, all are examples of moral or spiritual risks. Prayer is a risk. So is faith.

Note that risks are not defined by the activity. Learning to ski, for instance, could be a physical risk for some people and a social or emotional risk for others. It all depends on what's risky to you. If your concern is hurting yourself or testing your strength, then skiing is a physical risk, but if your concern is looking good to others, then skiing might be more of a social risk. If you don't like feeling out of control, then skiing might be an emotional risk. It's the meaning associated with the activity that determines the risk category.

Ask your children to come up with their own examples of risks for each category. Record their ideas in writing on paper or on the computer to go back to later.

If your children are teenagers, summarize with them what they think are the defining characteristics of each category as you talk about them. What does an intellectual risk look like? What makes an action a moral risk? Encourage them to think in terms of different age groups too. For instance, what might be a physical risk for a kindergartner? What about for a young adolescent? Or, an adult?

You might talk about how the nature of risk changes with age. What did they consider risky when they were younger that's not risky now? Similarly, what's become more risky to them as they've gotten older? Then, ask them what kind of risk taker they think they are.

What Kind of Risk Taker Are You?

Everyone has his or her own comfort level with each category of risk. Comfort levels change with age and experience too. Social risks, for instance, tend to be especially tough during adolescence and young adulthood, but become easier as we get older. Physical risks, on the other hand, typically become more challenging as we age.

Using a scale of 1–5 with 1 signifying the easiest and 5 the hardest, have each family member rank their comfort level for each category: intellectual, social, emotional, physical, and moral or spiritual. Use each number only once.

In this way each of you can evaluate your own pattern of risk-taking. When you're done, you'll know what kinds of risks appeal to you and which ones you tend to avoid.

Write your easiest category here:_____

Write your most challenging category here: _____

Which category was easiest to rank? _____

Which was most difficult? _____

When everyone is done ranking, talk about the experience. Were they surprised by any of their rankings? What did they think about as they did this?

You may be surprised at the responses of one or more of your children. Sometimes a child who seems very outgoing and popular may report that social risks are actually harder for her to take than some others. Or, the most physically active child may rank physical risks as one of his more difficult categories.

It also can be entertaining and enlightening to turn this into a game and try to guess each other's rankings, as well as your own. As an extension of this activity, your family could survey extended family members or friends regarding their rankings of risk categories, and look for trends across age, gender, or culture.

What Would Be a Risk for You?

Once your children have evaluated their own patterns of risk taking, ask them to choose one category to focus on and come up with at least seven things that would be a challenge for them in that category. It doesn't matter whether they choose their easiest or most difficult category; the point is to get them thinking about what's challenging to them, what causes them to feel apprehensive or a little anxious. You'll need to guide them, perhaps doing one or two together, because when people think of challenge, they often imagine the things that terrify them. It's OK to have one or two of those on the list, but it's more important to identify the things that make them a little anxious because it's by taking smaller risks that they'll gain the confidence they need to take bigger risks. Ask them to think about what makes them *a little apprehensive* or what causes them to feel *a bit nervous*.

For instance, many of us are afraid of public speaking. Just the idea of standing up in front of a group of people and talking for half an hour makes our palms sweat. When we imagine ourselves taking a risk like that we immediately see ourselves in the worst possible scenario. We see ourselves at a podium in front of an enormous auditorium filled with hundreds of our peers who have come to hear us talk. We visualize ourselves shaking in our shoes, flushed, sweating, and unable to recall a single thing we wanted to say. Sound familiar? That's a big risk, but it's not where I'm suggesting you ask your child to start.

Instead, think of related situations on a much smaller scale that might make your children feel just a little bit nervous. For example, what if the group consisted of only five people? Does the size of the group make a difference? How would that feel? What if your child was only speaking for 3 minutes? How nervous would she be then? What if she was simply introducing the main speaker? Does it matter if the audience consists of people she knows well or strangers? Some individuals are less nervous in front of people they'll never see again, while others feel more relaxed before familiar faces. A child who chooses the social category might come up with a list of seven risks that look like this:

- Going to play at the house of someone I don't know very well.
- Being the class helper/monitor.
- Singing in a talent show.
- Joining a drama group.
- Introducing myself to people I don't know.
- Sitting with different people at lunch.
- Raising my hand and asking a question.

The aim is to come up *with a range* of at least seven things that would feel risky to your child in one particular category, things that would make him just a little bit nervous, as well as things that would make him very anxious. The idea is to think about what it means to move out of a comfort zone toward the edge of competence.

REAL LIFE

Maggie, a seventh grader, chooses intellectual as her category because it's one she feels comfortable with. She's a good student and the first challenge she thinks of is taking algebra as an eighth grader. Math is her best subject and she could advance to algebra next year if she wanted to. Her math teacher has been encouraging her to consider it, and her parents want her to try it, but seems a big risk to Maggie because she's not sure how well she would do and getting an 'A' is important to her.

Other intellectual risks Maggie lists include doing the tougher, bonus problems her math teacher assigns, offering to tutor younger children, and speaking up more often in class when she has ideas about how to solve a problem. She adds that taking honors English next year also would be an intellectual risk because she's not as strong in reading and writing as she is in math.

Read the real-life example on this page for an illustration.

Your children should work together to help each other generate ideas for realistic challenges in their chosen category. Once your children have brainstormed at least seven risks for their chosen category, the second step is to make a plan for trying one challenge.

What Would Make It Easier?

Working at the edge of competence can unnerve us if we aren't prepared. It helps to have a plan. Ask your children what they could do to make the risk easier. Is there information they need or some skill they need to learn? Would it help to practice? What if they watched someone else do it first? Would it be easier if they took the risk with a friend, or with a group? Or, do they need to have privacy to take the risk? Would it help if they limited the time or gave themselves unlimited time? Maybe it would be easier if they gave themselves permission to not be perfect, or to be embarrassed, or even to fail.

For example, Max, a fifth grader, chose physical risks as his category. It's his favorite and easiest category. He loves sports and plays soccer and baseball. He came up with the following list of seven risks:

- Try out for a traveling soccer team.
- Play goalie.
- Play defense (he currently plays offense).
- Go to baseball camp.
- Try a new sport, like basketball.
- Start weight lifting.
- Play baseball with older kids.

When he considered what might make some of these risks easier to take, he acknowledged that it would be easy to go to camp if his good friend agreed to go too. Learning a new sport would be easier if he could learn some of the skills one-on-one with someone first, rather than in a group. He'd been thinking about weight lifting to improve his strength, and to do that he really needed someone to teach him. He'd be more likely to try it if he could do it with someone he knew and liked. His dad might be willing to teach him. As Max thought about it, he figured out several ways he could make each of his seven risks easier to take.

Have Fun Taking Risks

You can have a lot of fun taking risks as a family. Try to make it a habit. Start small if your children are young, or if they are resistant to stepping outside of their comfort zone. Aim to take one small, planned risk a week. But, if your children are older, if they enjoy reaching for challenge or making fun happen, aim to take one planned risk every 2 months or so. My experience has been that people of all ages find it challenging, meaningful, and fun to take a planned risk on a regular basis.

Children who have a high need to stay in their comfort zone(s) will take easy risks initially, but as they gain experience taking on a challenge and watch others who take on even greater challenges, they will be more willing to step out toward their own edge of competence. Each time your child takes a planned risk, her self-esteem will improve and she will view herself as more capable and resourceful. She will become more confident that she can meet new challenges.

Because people tend to put forth the most effort when they can take reasonable chances on things that matter to them most, let your child determine his own risks. Resist the temptation to suggest what kind of risk you think he should take. The exercise will be much more valuable if your child discovers on his own what works for him. The point is not that your child takes certain kinds of risks, but that he understands the relationship between risk and achievement and develops a desire to work at his edge of competence. You want your child to be routinely asking himself, "Where do I want to go with my life and how am I going to get there?"

Make sure you know ahead of time what risks your children have chosen. They need to be accountable to you. This way you can help them develop a plan that increases the likelihood that their risk is a positive experience. Most children take benign risks, cautiously stepping out of their comfort zone at first. The risks they choose to take reveal something about their self-perceptions, their anxieties, and their self-esteem.

For example, Rachel, a seventh grader, decided to sit with a different group of classmates at lunch for a week. Ten-year-old Jamal said he was going to learn to play the guitar. Shannai decided to try a back somersault off the high dive, and Doug enrolled in a month-long summer camp to learn a foreign language.

Most of the learning in facing a challenge comes from preparing to take the risk and in reflecting on it afterward. The discussion that you have with your children after they've taken on a challenge helps them identify what's most important and what may be getting in the way of reaching their highest aspirations.

Summary

Nobody improves by staying in his or her comfort zone. Your children have to be willing to take chances to achieve, and you must be willing to let them risk. High achievement requires a willingness to work at the edge of competence, the zone where they are uncertain of outcomes, where they have to stretch, and where they work alongside others with similar interests, abilities, and drive. It's a risky place.

Taking realistic risks is about recognizing things that make us a bit nervous and agreeing to walk through them. Each time your children take a risk, they increase their self-confidence, as well as their ability to take on a challenge. Encourage your children to experiment, to explore, and to consider possibilities, especially if these seem out of reach. They need to imagine themselves doing those things of which they dream.

Chapter Resources

Bloom, B. (Ed.). (1985). *Developing talent in young people.* New York: Ballantine Books.

Csikszentmihalyi, M. (1990). *Flow: The psychology of optimal experience.* New York: HarperCollins.

Gelb, M. J. (2003). *More balls than hands: Juggling your way to success by learning to love your mistakes.* New York: Penguin Group.

Ilardo, J. (1992). *Risk taking for personal growth.* Oakland, CA: Harbinger Publications.

Rimm, S. (1999). *See Jane win: The Rimm report on how 1,000 girls became successful women.* New York: Random House.

Walker, B. A., & Mehr, M. (1992). *The courage to achieve: Why America's brightest women struggle to fulfill their promise.* New York: Simon and Schuster.

—4—
Getting SMARTer About Goal Setting

Motivation is the art of getting people to perform necessary tasks they might not do on their own.

— William Warren, basketball coach and author

IF you made a New Year's resolution this year, chances are good you've already given up on it. The average length of time most of us keep a New Year's resolution is 3 weeks. We tell ourselves, "I'm going to get in shape," or "I'm going to lose weight," but we make little progress because the goals we set aren't very SMART.

SMART goals bring out the best in people. They are:
- **S**pecific,
- **M**easurable,
- **A**ttainable,
- **R**ealistic, and
- **T**imely.

Dreams are not goals.

 DOI: 10.4324/9781003237068-4

Goals are the daily action plan we follow to carry us toward our dreams. To realize dreams, we must set high but realistic goals and then look for and acknowledge progress toward those goals.

The higher the level of achievement your children aim for, the more crucial it becomes that their goals are well-defined. Developing their abilities means being able to clearly communicate, "This is the goal. This is how you get there."

Goals affect performance and motivation in three ways. They
- focus attention,
- influence persistence, and
- energize people.

Goals *focus our attention* by directing it toward activities that are relevant to the task and away from activities that are irrelevant. Goals *influence persistence* by their difficulty. Generally, more challenging goals increase persistence, provided that children have some control over the amount of time they have available to work on the goal. Goals also tend to *energize* people, thus increasing effort. This is why you must keep your expectations high for your children and help them learn how to set challenging goals for themselves.

Practical Help

If your capable child is struggling, you may be tempted to lower your expectations. A lot of us don't like to see our kids distressed. Lowering our expectations generally is a bad idea, though, because it tends to reduce children's effort and quietly communicates a vote of no confidence. If you believe that your child has the ability to do the work, keep your high expectations and offer lots of empathy, encouragement, and support when they are struggling. Say things like,

I can see that this is tough for you. I'm proud of the effort you're making.

I know this is a difficult time, and I'm confident you can do it.

This is hard and we'll get through it. We'll help you all we can.

How do we help our children set better goals to enhance their performance? We do it by communicating well-defined standards for their achievement ourselves and by coaching them to refine their own personal aims. In the real-life example, notice how Jonathan's parents coached him to set attainable goals.

Let's refine a popular goal together to see how you can make your goals SMARTer.

Many of us set goals to improve our health or fitness. Some of us start going to the gym; others walk with friends every day; some people cut back on sweets or portion sizes. Yet, looking at the statistics on obesity, Type II diabetes, and heart disease, it's clear we're not successful. We don't succeed because our goals aren't SMART. We set goals like:

- I'm going to exercise more.
- I'm going to eat better.
- I'm going to eat less.
- I'm going to get more sleep.

REAL LIFE

Our 11-year-old son, Jonathan, came home in a near panic over a complicated assignment that was due in 3 weeks. He wanted to do very well on it and was frantic about how much he would need to do to complete it. We had him sit down with a calendar and break the project down into specific, doable daily goals. When he finished, he seemed genuinely surprised that each of the daily goals was easy, and even more surprised that the assignment could actually get done ahead of schedule. He has a chapter test coming up in math in a few weeks and we saw him attack this in the same way, filling out his planner with daily goals to prepare. This helped us realize that he needs to learn how to break things down into smaller tasks; otherwise he gets overwhelmed and avoids doing anything because the projects seem too huge.

These are all good ideas, but they're not SMART. Take the first one: I'm going to exercise more. This goal is not specific. What kind of exercise are you going to do? It's also not measurable. There's no way to monitor progress. How often are you going to do it and for how long?

SMART fitness goals look like these:

- I'm going to walk for an hour, 4 days a week after dinner.
- I'm going to use the machines at the gym and keep my heart rate in its target zone for at least 30 minutes, 4 days a week.
- I'm going to join a soccer league with Philip and make 90% of the practices and games.

Notice how each of these goals includes something that can be counted. In the first example, it's the time and the number of days per week. In the second example, it's the heart rate, number of minutes, and number of days per week. In the last example, it's the number of soccer practices and games.

Let's try one more together and then we'll look at how to help our children set SMART goals. Take the goal, *I'm going to eat better,* make it more specific and measurable, and write it below.

_____

_____

_____

_____

_____

_____

_____

Were you able to refine the goal so you had something specific to measure? Here are some you may have come up with:

- I'm going to eat only one sweet thing a day.
- I'm going to cut back on sweets by eating only two desserts a week.
- I'm going to drink more water by taking a liter container of water to work and drinking it twice before I go home for the day.
- I'm going to limit fast food to twice a week.

Our children are just like us. They dream big, but they don't set SMART goals. They vow:

- I'm going to study more (or harder).
- I'm going to play varsity.
- I want to win.
- I want that scholarship.

Unless their goals are SMART, they're not likely to achieve them. Your role is to help teach them, through your communication and your example, how to take a long-range dream and break it down into weekly or daily objectives. If the goals your children set are SMART, and they get weekly feedback on the progress they're making toward them, you'll see a big boost in their effort, motivation, and achievement.

To get them started, ask them questions that focus on the steps they need to take to reach their goal, questions like:

- What do you think needs to happen to improve your grades?
- What do you think you need to change about how you study?
- What would increase your chances of winning?

- What can you do to save more money?

Your questions can help them clarify a vision and establish an action plan that improves their effort and motivation and dramatically increases the likelihood that they'll accomplish what they set out to do.

Long-term goals should be broken down so that it's possible to attain goals fairly quickly and get feedback regularly. Everyone needs feedback regarding their performance toward specific goals in order to adjust their effort or strategy. Without feedback, we have no way of knowing how we are doing.

Some parents are comfortable teaching their children directly. If that describes you, then you can help your kids by providing direct instruction in the use of the acronym SMART to revise and review goals weekly.

In the example on the next page, you'll see how one couple recognized the importance of letting their kids set their own goals in areas of interest to them, while at the same time encouraging their children to set goals in broader areas, as well.

Goals that are specific and measurable still can be lousy goals, however, if they're not realistic, attainable, or timely. Goals are not realistic or attainable unless your child has already demonstrated a similar level of success that suggests the goal is within her reach. If a child has never played volleyball, for instance, it's highly unlikely that she's going to make the top team. It's also unlikely that an average student is going to make the honor roll in a semester, or that a child with no musical training is going to become proficient with an instrument in a few months.

Don't discourage your kids from dreaming big. Simply help them keep the dream alive while focusing on the short-range targets.

REAL LIFE

Many years before we had children, we would talk at the beginning of the year and set some goals. This is something that we hope our children will do, so we thought we would seize the opportunity and show them what it looks like for us. There are things that we want to do, and we all know that they don't just happen.

We were just beginning to talk about the Christmas holiday and what we hoped would happen so we thought it was the perfect time. Both of the kids are old enough now to understand the process and the reasons behind doing it.

So, at dinner one night in November we introduced the idea and told them that we would talk about goals in a couple of days. We shared that we would be addressing four different areas of our lives and asked them to think about it and we would come up with our "list" on Friday. Toward the end of dinner on Friday, we broke out the paper and pen and our daughter wrote it all down. We categorized our goals into Spiritual, Personal, Family, and Holiday. The personal category included health and fitness, school grades, business, hobbies, etc. Family goals generally included the things that we would all be doing or would affect us all such as vacations, house projects and community service work. Holiday goals focused on Christmas and what we hoped to accomplish and enjoy.

It went very well. There was no complaining and actually, quite a bit of enthusiasm. Our plan is to do this quarterly. And, we can't wait to hear, "Yeah, we got that done! Ooo, and that too!"

What can they aim for this month and this week that will move them a step closer to their dream?

Timing is important too. Some goals are much more likely to be achieved if they are pursued when the time is right. Andrew, for instance, is a talented 11-year-old soccer player. He wants to try out for his city's elite traveling team. His goal is realistic—he has demonstrated the talent—but it's not timely, because he's not independent or mature enough yet for the responsibilities and pressures that come with traveling out of town every week with older boys. His parents and his coach support his goal, but they all believe the timing will be better in a year.

Similarly, Azreena's longstanding goal has been to attend a pre-professional training camp for aspiring musicians. She's been saving her money and has enough to enroll, but this year her mother has been going through cancer treatments and Azreena, understandably, doesn't want to be gone this summer. She decides to defer for a year because the timing's not right this year.

Even the character traits we desire for our children can be translated into SMART goals. We want them to be responsible, kind, honest, fair, and persevering, and to take initiative, for example. Here is what some desirable character traits look like as SMART goals:

For This Character Trait	Say
Be more responsible.	Put your toys away after playing.
Don't give up.	Practice 20 minutes, 5 times a day.
Work hard.	Spend 30 minutes every day on that task.
Take some initiative.	Do this every day without being asked.
Be honest.	Let me know when you make a mistake.
Be kind.	Do something for someone else every day.

There's one more thing you need to know before we look at some practical strategies to help children set SMART goals. Generally, it's best to avoid setting goals for your children that involve earning a score of some kind, like a certain time, speed, or grade. Instead, set goals that focus their attention on using some skill or strategy they've learned. In other words,

Don't Say	Say
Make the honor roll.	Complete all assigned homework.
Get a B on your science test.	Review for 10 minutes every night this week.
Play that piece with no mistakes.	Practice the hardest measures for 10 minutes every day.
Win the game.	Make 75% of your free-throw shots.

Confident kids will work harder toward challenging goals set by their coaches, teachers, and parents. Kids who believe that they can achieve will set more challenging goals for themselves, as well. Self-assured children demonstrate a greater commitment to their goals, and accept and use negative feedback more positively than do less confident children. Therefore, one of your aims as a parent should be to help your children build their self-confidence.

Kids develop this assurance in three ways:
- by experiencing success,
- by identifying with someone who is confident, and
- by being inspired by someone who believes in him or her.

Notice in the example on the next page how a talented swimmer gets a dose of all three from her coach.

REAL LIFE

My daughter's swim coach suggested she work to meet a certain category of times in order to participate in a very big meet late this summer. At first, she wasn't that interested in making that meet, but I noticed that the weekly goal her coach set got her paying attention to her times.

At swim meets, her coach talked to her right before and immediately after each event. He told her what was good about her performance, and what she needed to work on improving. I eavesdropped a few times and what surprised me is how he downplayed winning and rank. He really focused on shaving a second or two off at each meet, knowing that it would add up to a significant change over several months. After about a month of weekly goals, I heard my daughter decide that she wanted to participate in the meet at the end of the summer.

When Abrianna joined the team, the coach put her in the competitive group, even though she'd have to work hard to stay there. She rose to the challenge and worked very hard. Even so, most of the time she was the slowest in any set. Her coach talked to her every week, reminding her that she's the youngest in that group, is new to the sport, and still has a lot of growing ahead of her. Abrianna was elated the first time she managed to do all of the laps the other swimmers in her group did. We celebrated! It makes me proud to see her keep working hard, even though she's often last.

Do you see how the girl in the example experiences success every week? Even though she comes in last place, she wins every week when she reaches her personal goals. Her parents and her coach communicate their confidence in her ability to succeed by encouraging her to work at the very edge of her competence. She's in the competitive group. It's tough and it's risky, but you can imagine the impact that has on this high-potential kid. It says,

- You have what it takes.
- We see that you could be great one day.
- We believe in you.

Placement in the competitive group also provides Abrianna with a number of slightly older, more experienced, motivated swimmers to identify with. Every day she observes others who are confident and working just as hard as she is, if not harder.

And, did you notice the ways her parents and coach inspired Abrianna? Her parents celebrated the small accomplishments that represented big gains for her. They understand that during this season of very hard work, there will be no awards, no applause, and no public recognition. She will work hard 6 days a week for an entire summer, for what? To make progress that will establish a foundation from which she can launch a bigger success. That's what. So, they make a big deal of the relative big successes. Their celebrations help to mark her "success."

Her coach also realizes the importance of immediate feedback and the need to keep her focused on her progress and off her "defeats." She can compare herself to her competitors and always see herself as coming up short, or she can compare her performance this week with her performance last week and be proud of the gains she has made. Her coach talks to her after every race to make sure she does the latter. His comments inspire confidence and, as a result, she keeps trying.

Find ways to engage your children in activities they enjoy that provide some challenge while giving them success. Make sure they're reaching for and have the support they need to hit their weekly targets. Give feedback that affirms their strengths, while encouraging them to work at the edge of their competence:

- You have a very good memory. Soon you'll have that entire sonata memorized.
- You've put a lot of effort into your art. I think you're ready for the next class.
- You learned that play fast. Let's try something more challenging.

You have to know what your children's passions are. In what would they be willing to wholeheartedly invest themselves? What are they most motivated to pursue? If you're not sure, one surefire way to find out is to ask them this question:

If you were guaranteed success, what would your dream be?

You can mull this question over during a ride in the car, over a family dinner together (everybody gets a turn to answer it), or while sitting or walking together. Better yet, pose it and give them a day or two to respond.

Be careful that whenever you're talking with your kids about the important things in life you have a dialogue, not a lecture. Don't ask questions or evaluate your child's response. Just listen and make an occasional comment that invites her to tell you more, such as:

- That's very interesting.
- I didn't know that about you.
- I'm really glad I asked the question.
- Say more about that.

Another way to get at your children's interests and dreams is to have everyone in the family make a list of their dreams using the worksheet that follows. This can be fun to share as a family, as well.

List of Dreams

Make a list of 80 things you'd like to do in your lifetime if you had all the money, health, and friends and education you wanted. No limits. What would be on your list?

_____   _____

_____   _____

_____   _____

_____   _____

_____   _____

_____   _____

_____   _____

_____   _____

_____   _____

_____   _____

_____   _____

_____   _____

_____   _____

_____   _____

_____   _____

_____   _____

_____   _____

_____   _____

WORKSHEET

WORKSHEET

_____   _____
_____   _____
_____   _____
_____   _____
_____   _____
_____   _____
_____   _____
_____   _____
_____   _____
_____   _____
_____   _____
_____   _____
_____   _____
_____   _____
_____   _____
_____   _____
_____   _____
_____   _____

REAL LIFE

Jeanne and Doug's ambitious, 13-year-old son, Beckett, is a bright kid with several learning challenges. "He's ADHD," explains his mother, "and has a mild learning disability in reading, so school isn't easy for him. He needs a lot of support to stay focused and organized." Consequently, one of Beckett's weekly goals always has to do with organization.

"This is his first year in middle school and it's much tougher for him to stay on top of what's expected. He has trouble keeping track of what's due when and for whom."

To help him develop the habit of communicating with his teachers and seeking feedback, one of Beckett's goals is to ask his teachers on Mondays, Wednesdays, and Fridays about current and upcoming assignments. Then, with his parents' help, he makes a plan for how he'll get the work done in the days ahead.

"It's not perfect by a long shot," says Beckett's father, "but it's a start. Often, he asks, but doesn't get all the information he needs, or he gets the information, and then loses it. It can be pretty frustrating. It's a learning process for all of us and I have to learn to be patient with him. He's doing the best he can."

Success breeds success. It's important that your children learn to struggle, but make sure that your children have more success than failure experiences. They should have enough challenge to keep them making an effort and to experience some disappointments and setbacks, but challenge that's realistic and attainable enough that they experience success regularly.

Remember that the simple act of assigning a challenging goal can raise a child's confidence because it communicates an expectation and a confidence that the individual has the ability to accomplish the task. That's why it's important to keep the bar high while providing support and guidance.

Take Time to Review

Goals dim if they aren't polished up once in a while. Your children need to review their goals often to keep focused on them. They need feedback about their performance toward specific goals at least once a week in order to adjust their effort or strategy. Otherwise, they have no way of knowing how they are doing. One of the reasons that Weight Watchers has been so effective as a weight loss program for so many people is because there are weekly meetings where participants have a confidential weigh-in to track their progress. They get frequent feedback on their progress toward the goal they set at the beginning of the program.

Most businesses and corporations require their managers to make weekly or monthly reports on their progress toward production or sales goals. And, your child's weekly music lesson or sports match is used by his teacher or coach to assess his progress or lack of it toward certain goals. Anyone who is serious about realizing a dream regularly reviews their progress on their goals.

Break It Down

You can help your child learn how to chunk a big goal into edible bites. One way is to break it down for them and tell them what the daily and weekly goals are, as we saw in the swim coach example previously. Another option is to guide your children in the process by asking them a series of questions. The worksheet on pages 76–77 will help you do this.

REAL LIFE

Meta is a motivated 12-year-old whose parents often feel as though they can barely keep up with her. Her mother says, "She's interested in everything and has so much energy. It's go, go, go with her! Sometimes I get tired just listening to her!"

Meta's parents are confident that their daughter will continue to achieve, but they also want to do what they can to help her realize her dreams. Meta's father says, "She's a dreamer. I love that about her. But, I'm more of a realist. I know that it takes more than wishing and working hard to make some dreams come true. She needs to have a plan."

So, Meta's parents help her set goals. They do this by modeling and coaching. As a family, they set monthly and weekly goals. They're not always consistent, but they try to remember to review their goals weekly. Like many families, they spend a lot of time in the car, going from one kid's ball game to another. They find that riding in the car or watching a game together are the easiest times available to review goals. They'll ask, "How did your goals go this week?" Meta has learned that her parents are interested in more than an "OK," or "good" answer. They want specifics.

They model that when they reflect on their progress or lack of it on their own goals. Meta's mom, for instance, helps teach Hebrew class on Saturday mornings and has decided to do some of the memory work with her students. She set a goal of learning two new verses a week, or about one passage a month. When she reflects on her week's progress, she says, "I memorized two new verses and I still know the four I learned the past 2 weeks. I've reviewed every day in the shower." Or, if she hasn't reached her goal, she might say, "I only memorized one verse this week. It was harder for me this week, I think, because I have a lot going on at work and I've been distracted in the mornings when I usually review."

Breaking Goals Down

One way to break goals down to make them more manageable for children is to ask a series of questions. Follow the instructions below to help your kids break down some of their goals.

First, ask your child: "What's one thing you'd really like to accomplish this year?" Have him or her write his or her answer in the center of the bullseye below.

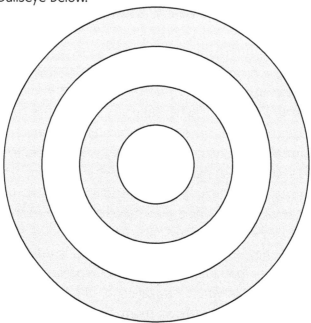

Then ask, "What three things have to happen in order for you to do that?" Have him or her write each one in the spaces provided below:

_____

_____

_____

_____

_____

_____

When he or she has listed three, say, "Now choose one of those three and list six things that you'd have to do to make that happen."

1. _____

_____

2. _____

_____

3. _____

_____

4. _____

_____

5. _____

_____

6. _____

_____

W O R K S H E E T

When your child is finished, discuss which one of these should be done first, and then ask your child if he or she would be willing to start this week. Chances are good he or she will say yes, but if not, you could ask, "When would you be willing to begin?" or "What do you think you would need to get started?" Write down your child's answers and hold onto them as a motivating factor to get started.

Summary

If you ever tried to get somewhere when you didn't know exactly where you were going, you probably ended up someplace else. Talent without goals won't take us to our destination. Goals are the daily action plan that takes your children to their dreams. The ability to set SMART goals is a skill every child needs to learn. SMART goals are **S**pecific, **M**easurable, **A**ttainable, **R**ealistic, and **T**imely. Your children need your guidance to help them understand what steps are involved in reaching higher goals because they lack experience building gradually toward some specific outcome.

Chapter Resources

Locke, E. A., & Latham, G. P. (1984). *Goal setting: A motivational technique that works!* Englewood Cliffs, NJ: Prentice Hall.

Tracy, B. (2004). *Goals! How to get everything you want—Faster than you thought possible.* San Francisco: Berret-Koehler Publishers.

Every Dream Begins With a Picture

Improving Performance With Mental Rehearsal

MORGAN is frustrated. He knows he can play this Chopin prelude much better than he just did. When he practices at home he plays it beautifully. There, in the privacy of his family's living room, the piece makes his heart sing. But, each week he experiences the same letdown when he plays for his teacher. When she's seated on her stool to his left, his nerves get in the way of his playing this simple composition at his best. He never plays as well for her as he does for himself. How can he be more consistent in his performance?

Every achievement begins with a picture.

Think about it. When you struggled to learn to swim as a child, what motivated you to keep trying? Wasn't it that image you had in your head of yourself gliding easily through the water, making it all the way to the diving board from which you saw your parents or friends admiring your fearless cannonballs into the deep water, and the sense of pride and joy real enough to keep yourself going as you struggled for air?

 DOI: 10.4324/9781003237068-5

What about as you got older? What kept you working hard at a sport, or at an instrument? Wasn't it that image you had of yourself before a crowd of admirers, performing beyond everyone's expectations—making the three pointer that saves the game, playing a difficult series of arpeggios flawlessly, or doing the small acts of service behind the scenes that make the difference between a lackluster event and an outstanding experience for everyone else?

Because we become what we imagine, it's essential to imagine the best.

Mental rehearsal means to practice in your head. The research is clear that mental rehearsal is better than no practice at all. To perform in your head will improve your performance. Even better, mental rehearsal combined with physical practice is better than either alone. To really boost their performance, your children should do both. Mental rehearsal improves the mindsets associated with performance more than the physical skills. In other words, it has the biggest effect on your child's confidence, attitude, focus, and concentration.

Mental rehearsal could help Morgan a lot. He already is an accomplished pianist. He performs for an audience several times a year and he is a competitive student; he wants to do well. Learning to stay relaxed, confident, and focused is something mental rehearsal is especially good for. However, to use visualization, Morgan has to be able to imagine himself playing. He has to be able to hold that image and control it in order to use this technique to improve. That will take practice.

Getting Started

Mental rehearsal is not a good substitute for real practice. But, when children are well-prepared, it can provide a substantial boost to performance. By learning to practice in their heads, your children can train themselves to feel more confident and self-controlled in difficult situations.

To get your kids started, try one of the simple games described below. Regardless of your children's level of ability, these will help.

Mental Filming

Mental rehearsal requires recall of specific behaviors that facilitate a great performance. One way to build a storage bank of "photos" of good performances is to watch those who are better than you are at something you want to improve. For instance, let's say your child wants to become a better snowboarder. He wants to keep his knees bent, stay centered, and maintain his balance. He wants to pick a line with confidence. If your child looks for others about his own age who do this well and chooses one or two to watch closely, he can begin to memorize images of what it looks like to do it well.

Sharper Image

Another way your children can improve their ability to recall what they want to imagine is to practice attending to and recalling visual images. Ask them to quietly sit on the floor or in a chair directly in front of a good friend. Tell them to close their eyes and try to capture the sharpest possible image they can of the other person. Encourage them to imagine all of the details of their face and movements. Allow a full minute, or 30 seconds if they're under the age of 9. Then, invite them to imagine the other person talking and to try to capture the sound of his or her voice. Imagine the other person's expressions too. Allow another 30–60 seconds. Finally, tell them to

REAL LIFE

Seven-year-old Shelly learned to dive last summer. This summer, she wants to be able to swim out to the dock at the lake so she can dive off of it with her older sister. The dock is farther out in deep water than she's ever swam before so she's a bit nervous about it, but she's watched her sister do it so many times it's easy to imagine herself doing it too. To build her confidence, Shelly's parents helped her prepare a mental rehearsal. Now, every night, Shelly "swims to the dock" in her mind before she goes to sleep.

Fourteen-year-old Travis is really good with words. He loves to debate and hopes to try out for his high school's debate team next year. To get ready, he attends the high school debate meets when he can and watches some of the best debaters. Watching them, he's learned that how a point is argued is just as important, if not more important, than what is actually said. Now, when Travis imagines himself debating next year, he sees himself using some of the same gestures and speech mannerisms as the team's top performers.

notice all of the feelings they have about their friend. Then tell them to open their eyes and look closely at one another, taking note of what they missed in their imagination. Let them comment on what they now notice that they will add next time they take a snapshot in their mind. Play this game a couple of times a week with your children to strengthen their attention and visual recall ability.

The ability to form sharp images and to control those images affects how well individuals can visualize. Most people can form the image in their mind, but usually they don't control it very well initially. They don't see themselves successfully performing the task. Instead, they see themselves making mistakes. The higher the achievement and the higher the stakes involved, the more practice it takes to control the images. Children who can form the images and control them well will achieve a lot. Our next game, Scene Switch, is an exercise designed to help your children increase their control of their images.

Scene Switch

There's nothing mystical about this switching procedure. It's just a skill for improving children's ability to mentally rehearse desired achievements. It works on developing their ability to bring images to mind when they need them.

1. Pick a quiet, undisturbed place for your children to sit and use the exercises they learned in Chapter 2 to get fully relaxed and focused.
2. Ask them to imagine a favorite scene that is familiar and calm, maybe a favorite vacation spot, favorite walk, or a favorite time of day. Tell them to imagine vivid details of that scene, capturing the colors, the sounds, and the smells. They are to fill the scene with as much sensory detail as they can. Have them stay with the scene for a couple of minutes, to allow their senses to experience as much of the scene as they can while remaining relaxed physically.
3. When they have this wonderful picture in their mind, sharply detailed and vivid, tell them to freeze-frame it. Direct them to lock it in place and turn it off. Then they are to go back to their controlled breathing and focus on their relaxation. Have them keep the scene turned off for 2 minutes.
4. Direct them to bring the scene to mind again. They are to imagine the same scene with all of the details and pleasant emotions they experienced before. Have them spend 2–3 minutes enjoying this scene before turning it off again and focusing once more on their relaxed breathing.

Remember that mental rehearsal is not a good substitute for actual practice. No amount of mental rehearsal will be effective if your children haven't bothered to practice. Mental rehearsal is intended as a supplementary tool to boost performance, not as a replacement for actual practice. Also, mental rehearsal is proven to be more effective when people practice every day.

To make the most of mental rehearsal, your children have to know what it is that they want to rehearse. That's why goal setting comes before mental rehearsal. The more specific they can be detailing their goals, the stronger and more effective they can make their mental rehearsals. Do they want to speak without hesitating? Do they want to complete a test or audition with confidence and poise? Do they want to play or sing a piece of music without making a mistake? Do they want to be able to maintain their concentration for a couple of hours? Once they know what it is they want to accomplish they can determine a visualization to rehearse it.

Begin With a Picture in Mind

Each of us is most motivated to give our best effort in the things that interest us most, so begin there. What do your children really like to do?

Ask them to describe an ideal performance. What would it look like if they

- Skied a great run?
- Studied hard?
- Did their best on a test?
- Played their instrument very well?
- Nailed that presentation?

Probe for as many details as you can, especially sensory details. Adding details of color, sounds specific to their performance situation, and all of the surrounding environmental features will increase the effectiveness of their mental rehearsal. Ask them to imagine they're watching a video recording of themselves giving a great performance of anything they'd like to be able to repeat. What do they see? Hear? Feel?

Another strategy for getting this information from your kids is to say: "Let's say we have magic dust that can make changes in anything over which it is sprinkled. What would you want to change about your performance in _____? Be specific."

This strategy can be applied to simple, everyday achievements, as well. For example, when asked what he would want to change about his piano performance, Morgan says, "I'd sit down at the piano and my mind would be on nothing but the music. I'd feel relaxed and looking forward to playing. My feet would be flat on the ground, and then I'd lift my right foot and place it lightly on the right pedal. My heart wouldn't race and I'd take a few deep breaths. My shoulders would be relaxed, too, and my wrists loose. I'd enjoy it. I wouldn't make any mistakes and I'd play the way I do at home when nobody's watching. My teacher would be really pleased with how I did, and the applause would be loud. It would be fun."

You can build your child's awareness of the characteristics associated with his best and less than best achievements if each time you see him give what is for him a great performance, you reinforce it as such and help him note what made his achievement so good. Here's another real-life example.

REAL LIFE

Mia, a talented fourth grader with attention difficulties, is inconsistent with her homework. Occasionally, she completes all of it and makes a good effort, but more often her work is incomplete. She often starts but doesn't finish.

When Mia is asked to think about her "best homework performance," she bites her lip and takes a moment to reflect. Then she brightens as she recalls a night not too long ago when she got all of her math homework done in record time. Asked to pretend that she has a video recording of herself giving that "performance," Mia says that she was seated at the dining room table with only her math book, her pencil, and a piece of paper. Her father was in the kitchen, fixing dinner, and her mother and siblings weren't home yet. There was a TV program that she really wanted to watch, so she had a timer set for 20 minutes in front of her because she needed to finish the work in that amount of time in order to watch her program. When she finished before the timer, her father checked her work and she remembers smiling because all of her answers were correct.

As she talked about it, Mia said that she thought that having a timer and a deadline—something interesting to get to next—helped her to keep her focus. She also thought it helped that her siblings weren't around. "When they're around, they're noisy and I can't think," she said.

Mia was encouraged to try repeating the components of that "great performance" the next time she did her homework:

- To work with a deadline and a timer.
- To work alone without any distractions and keep just the work she's attending to in front of her.
- To work toward some reward that she can earn quickly.
- To have a parent check her work before she turns it in.

By remembering what her best performances look like, Mia can learn to repeat her best achievements by recreating the same scenario. She won't always be successful because she's young. Learning to imagine vividly and to control those images takes time and practice.

Building a Mental Rehearsal

Relaxation is key to mental rehearsal, so don't begin teaching your children how to mentally rehearse until you are confident that they are able to relax their bodies (see Chapter 2).

Once your children can relax easily and have some capacity to control the pictures they imagine, you can begin to systematically build a mental rehearsal that will boost their performance in almost anything they want to do better.

Remember to begin by clarifying what it is that they want to improve. Do they want to:

- stay focused?
- remain calm under pressure?
- stay relaxed?
- feel more confident?
- nail that dismount?
- practice every day?

Imagine the target. Decide ahead of time what mood your children should be in to give their best performance. If they do their best when they're calm, then they need to practice imagining themselves calm. If they get better outcomes when they're supercharged or a bit excited or nervous, then they should imagine that. Energy is associated with strong feelings, so it's sometimes helpful to convert

REAL LIFE

Sixteen-year-old Alexia is using the same mental rehearsal techniques that helped her improve her performance in the quarter mile to enhance her performance on the college admission test she'll take this year.

"When I run a quarter mile, I concentrate on something different for each leg of it. Like on the back stretch, I focus on striding it out and on the second turn I concentrate on driving through. In the last leg I just keep telling myself, 'hold your form; hold your form.' It's the same thing with my SAT. There are different sections to the test and each section presents a different kind of challenge."

Just as she has a routine for every race, Alexia is developing a routine for this important exam. "I'm using mental rehearsal to imagine myself doing exactly what I need to do on each section to give it my best."

the energy associated with those feelings into effort toward a task.

When you and your children are clear about the behavior or attitude they want to polish, go ahead with the following exercises. If the object of their practice is something that can be videotaped, then by all means record their performances whenever you can. Not only will watching videos enhance their ability to "see" themselves in their mind's eye, but it also will document their progress. Then, on days when they are feeling discouraged or frustrated about their progress, take a few minutes to review some older tapes with them and point out how much they've improved. Sometimes when we're in the midst of hard work toward a long-term goal, we lose perspective on how far we've come. Taking a few moments to reflect and actually look at where we've been can do a lot to boost our motivation and keep our sights on the goal. The simple strategies that follow will help your children shift to more positive expectations and outcomes in their performance.

Rewind

Invite your child to sit down, close her eyes, and relax. Direct her to practice her controlled breathing for a full minute before you begin. Then, pausing between directions, say the following:

> Imagine yourself doing something you enjoy that you would like to do better. It can be anything . . . (long pause) . . . Notice how you feel as you are doing it. Are you tense? Relaxed? Excited? . . . In your mind, watch yourself do this activity . . . Slow the picture down enough that you can see and hear the details—how your feet or hands are moving, the changing expressions on your face, what others are saying, etc. (wait 2 minutes before you continue) . . . When you see yourself make a mistake, stop the picture and rewind it. Then replay it, slowing the action down as if you were watching a video frame by frame. Correct the mistake and return the speed of your imagined film to normal speed.

Scene Switch II

This exercise increases the complexity of the images your child visualized in the earlier exercise. Have your child relax as before using controlled breathing. Then proceed by giving your child the following directions. Be sure to allow plenty of time between directives for your child to imagine the scene.

1. Pay attention to your favorite scene for 2–3 minutes, participating fully with all your senses. Then turn it off for 2 minutes, and focus only on your relaxed breathing.
2. Now imagine a skill you wish to improve: a presentation, a pitch, a conversation, a competition, etc. See yourself as the participant, not an observer. This is very important. Picture yourself doing exceptionally well. Feel the emotions that come over you as you give your best performance. Hear the applause or cheers and compliments that arise. See the smiles and clapping hands,

REAL LIFE

Eleven-year-old Hans is competitive about everything. Whatever he does, he wants to excel. So, it was no surprise when his class held a fundraising event to help disaster victims that he was motivated to raise the most money. But, Hans' dad says, "It was a problem for him because the fundraising involved selling and this is something that Hans isn't too keen on. He didn't like the idea of going door-to-door soliciting, even though he was passionate about the cause. It was just a matter of knowing how to handle different situations that might arise when he went to a stranger's door."

Hans' father helped him develop a mental rehearsal that built his confidence for selling. "It didn't take us long to create the mental rehearsal. Then he practiced it every day for about 2 weeks before the fundraiser began and every day during it as well. I think it made a difference because Hans sold more magazines than anyone in his class."

the pats on the back, and all of the support and well-wishing that comes with such an achievement. Make these images as vivid as you can. Then, freeze frame those feelings.

3. Switch back to the relaxed scene. Breathe deeply and increase your feelings of relaxation for at least 2 minutes. Then, turn the wonderful achievement scene back on again. Notice all of the details—what you hear and see, what you can touch. Take in all of the positive emotions of a job well done. Picture yourself as clearly as you can and fully participate with all of your senses.

Practice this switching exercise every day for about 20 minutes, and direct your children to gradually increase the time they spend imagining their desired achievement.

Here's a modification on this exercise that varies your children's viewpoint on their performance. In the previous exercise, they saw themselves as the participant. In this exercise, they watch themselves as an observer. Here's what you say:

> This time as you imagine your performance, watch yourself from a distance of several yards away. How do you look? Are you relaxed? Confident? Having a good time? Notice your expression, what you do with your hands, your posture, your movements. Take in all of the details of your performance. Now shift the scene, taking the viewpoint of the participant, as if you are watching from inside yourself. Again note how you feel, how you look, and how you sound from this perspective.

When you're finished, compare the two viewpoints with your child. Which one was easier to take? In what way was the experience different when he shifted perspective?

Managing Distractions and Setbacks

A few early failures in life take the pressure off an undefeated record.
—unknown sportswriter

Whatever your child's passion, if she's on the road to the highest levels of achievement, she will encounter setbacks. Kids get sick or get injured; equipment fails; the weather is bad; coaches and teachers change. Your child is not going to place in every race, score every game, ace every test, or be applauded every time she shows up. If she's working at the edge of her competence and taking realistic risks, she will experience disappointments and rejections from time to time. If she's unprepared, your child's first setback could really throw her when it comes along. Setbacks are easier to work through if you expect them and prepare for them. This is true for you, as well as your child.

Mental rehearsal can help. Here's what you need to keep in mind and be ready to communicate to your child:

- Setbacks will happen. They will happen many times in your life. Expect them and prepare for them psychologically.
- Remember that when setbacks occur, people need time to recover, sometimes physically, as well as emotionally. Keep the big picture in mind. Your child (and you) will recover if you give yourself time.
- Do not equate your child's self-worth to his achievements. Ground his identity and self-esteem in who he is as a person, not on what he accomplishes.
- Go easy on your child when setbacks happen. Recovery and repair take time.

You can help your children persevere through setbacks by first anticipating what they might look like for your children. Robyn, for instance, competes nationally in horse jumping. The list of potential things that can go wrong is one thing she plans for before competition. She says,

> I have a plan for the usual setbacks—what I'll do if I get sick, if my horse gets sick, if my horse balks at the gate or crashes into it, if it's really hot or rainy, or if a piece of equipment gets misplaced. There's so much that can go wrong that it doesn't make sense to prepare for each and every thing. Instead, we just assume that stuff will happen and I practice in my head what my reaction will be. Usually, my mental rehearsals involve staying calm, acknowledging what has happened, and quickly coming up with a plan for dealing with it. I always see myself calm and confident in my mind and going ahead with the event.

Tico is one of the best players on his Little League baseball team. Up until now, he's been very successful. This year, at the end of the season, he was selected to compete on the league's All Star team. It's a big honor. But now, all of the players on this team are as good as he is and the team is playing other communities' All Star teams. It's much more competitive. So far, Tico's performance on this team has been erratic. He says, "The problem is, when I make a mistake, I can't let it go. I keep thinking about what I should have done. I know it's no good, but I can't seem to stop myself. It's really messing with my game."

Tico is learning what many talented athletes, musicians, and artists know—that making a mistake can throw your performance if you dwell on it. Mental rehearsal can help Tico learn to manage these distractions and maintain his focus.

You can use mental rehearsal to improve your child's ability to cope with challenging or difficult scenarios. For instance, it's not uncommon for young talented children to have a low tolerance for frustration and to become upset when they're working problems that are challenging. Teachers see plenty of bright children who break down in tears and give up trying when they encounter a problem or a question that they can't answer at once. These children need to build their tolerance for difficulty. Mental rehearsal can help them learn to respond positively to their frustration. They might see themselves making encouraging self-statements, like, "OK, this is hard. If I stay with it, I'll figure it out," or "Slow down, take your time, and work it out." Or, they might see themselves relaxing their bodies and keeping their attention on the task.

If your children are planning for a high-stakes situation, say a competition, or an important test, audition, or interview, they can use mental rehearsal to imagine the things they fear might go wrong and shift the image in their mind to what they want to go right. The goal is to imagine themselves responding positively to the difficulty when it arises.

When's the Best Time to Use Mental Practice?

Many elite athletes report that they mentally practice in bed before they fall asleep. Many also use their mental blueprints during the actual event. About a third mentally rehearse about once a week on average, while about 10% do it every day. After dinner can be a good time to mentally rehearse because it's a time when many of us relax most easily. However, mental rehearsal can sometimes activate the mind, making it harder to fall asleep. Take advantage of your children's natural daily rhythms and encourage them to mentally rehearse when they are alert but relaxed enough to focus well.

Mental rehearsal is not something that you get good at in a few weeks. It must be mastered before its best results are achieved. Frequent practice is required to get observable results. Using it haphazardly is a waste of time.

Mental rehearsal works better for some people than others because we vary in our ability to hold mental images in our minds and to manipulate those images. Plan to introduce this skill to your children gradually, especially if they're young, and expect to build the skill over several years. As your children's mental capacities grow, so will their abilities to learn to rehearse mentally.

Summary

The popular saying, "Think positive," is supported by the research on imagery and mental rehearsal. Essentially anything your children would like to do better will be helped by mental rehearsal. Like other mental skills, mental rehearsal improves with practice. It's a waste of time to begin using this skill 2 days before a high-stakes evaluation or an important competition because it takes months to reap the benefits of this skill. Simple steps to mentally rehearse for young children involve practicing paying attention to the characteristics associated with their best performance. Kids also benefit from practice imagining visual images—stopping and starting them in their mind's eye. Because mastery is a matter of practice, the more opportunities you create for your children to practice, the better they will become at it. Mental rehearsal is especially good for improving a particular technique or skill, for preparing for competition, and for correcting a specific aspect of performance. It's like a mini-road map. It provides a picture of where one wants to go and how to get there.

Chapter Resources

Gallwey, T. (2000). *The inner game of work.* New York: Random House.

Greene, D. (2001). *Audition success: An Olympic sports psychologist teaches performing artists how to win.* New York: Routledge.

Greene, D. (2002). *Performance success: Performing your best under pressure.* New York: Routledge.

Ungerleider, S. (2005). *Mental training for peak performance.* New York: Rodale.

Ungerleider, S., & Golding, J. (1990). *Beyond strength: Psychological profiles of Olympic athletes.* New York: McGraw Hill.

—6—

In the Zone

*Using Mood Management
to Improve Achievement*

TALK with elite achievers who have to give an outstanding performance on demand and they will tell you that they know exactly what they need to do to get themselves "in the zone." It's not something they mess with. Whether it's starring in a leading role on stage, giving a concert, playing a game, or running a meeting, world-class achievers tend to be religious about their mood management. They can't afford not to.

Your children are not at that level yet, but that doesn't mean that they can't begin to profit from the knowledge and experience of thousands of elite performers. There's plenty to learn about how to exit and enter your optimal zone of achievement and some of it can be applied very early. Let's begin with some simple but effective strategies.

 DOI: 10.4324/9781003237068-6

Profiling Your Children's Energy

Under what conditions do your children do their best work? Are they morning people? If so, you probably notice the limits of their energy by mid- or late afternoon. If they're night people, they probably don't get really warmed up for work until afternoon or evening. Knowing the conditions that keep us mentally alert and energized and exploiting them to extend our limits is *mood management.* The goal is to be able to mobilize energy on demand. Your child's energy works as an exchange. He has to add to it and take away from it. Learning how to control this energy exchange involves learning how to:

- add energy effectively,
- minimize leaks and loss of energy, and
- spend energy efficiently.

Too many kids (and a lot of adults) stumble into an energy trough in the afternoon. If you help your children attend to their basic sources of energy, they can work less and achieve more. Parents can lead by creating an environment that supports the essential first steps.

Mood and the Brain

You help your children manage their mood when you know something about how the brain affects feelings. Four chemicals in the brain help regulate mood:

- serotonin,
- GABA,
- catecholamines, and
- endorphins.

One of these, serotonin, we'll discuss in detail, as it's one of the easiest to alter.

Serotonin is a neurotransmitter that is your primary defense against depression and anxiety. It's made from the amino acid tryptophan, which comes from animal protein, like dairy products and meat. Tryptophan is quickly converted in the body to 5-hydroxytryptophan (5-HTTP) and from that, to serotonin. When your children don't get enough protein, their bodies lack the tryptophan they need to keep serotonin levels at their best. They feel more irritable and have trouble concentrating. So, what can you do to keep their serotonin levels up?

An easy first step is to get them to eat 10–15 g (about 1 oz) of protein at breakfast instead of consuming all of their daily 60 g (6 oz) allowance at one or two meals.

Many children eat too little protein and too much sugar, a diet that promotes stress reactions that can lead to chronically elevated levels of the stress hormones. When children's breakfasts consist mostly of simple carbohydrates (e.g., boxed cereal, breads, sugared drinks) they lose energy and concentration by midmorning. Protein is the best fuel for mental effort the way complex carbohydrates are the best fuel for physical exertion. Add some protein to their breakfast.

Protein is metabolized a lot more slowly than simple carbohydrates, resulting in more stable blood sugar and insulin levels. When your children eat enough protein in the morning, they are able to focus and maintain their concentration longer without fatigue. They don't get hungry as quickly and they have more energy.

In addition, some children benefit by adding or substituting a small protein snack (e.g., an egg or a cheese stick) in the afternoon. When overweight children consume their protein in small amounts throughout the day, they also may discover that they lose weight over time because they're less likely to overeat at meals and to snack in between.

How can you get your children to make these changes? Begin with yourself. The greatest influence you have with your children is the example you set, so start with your own habits.

Would you be willing to try a simple experiment? Pay attention to your own energy levels over the next few days. Use the chart below and record a number to represent your overall energy level throughout different periods of the day, as indicated.

A 7 means that you're at your best. You feel alert, energized, and find it easy to concentrate. A 5 means you're doing well, but not at your peak levels. Record a 3 when you have to make a conscious effort to keep yourself going. You may be feeling hungry or fatigued, and may be having trouble keeping your mind on what you're doing. Record a 1 for those times when you're not good for much of anything except a meal, a nap, or zoning in front of the television.

Feel free to add or change the times to fit your personal schedule. You also can use any of the numbers between 1 and 7—for instance, if you're not quite a 7, but you're better than a 5, record a 6. Keep track of your energy levels for 3 work days.

	Day 1	**Day 2**	**Day 3**
8 a.m.			
10 a.m.			
12 p.m.			
2 p.m.			
4 p.m.			
6 p.m.			
8 p.m.			
10 p.m.			

Kyra's Chart

	Day 1	Day 2	Day 3
8 a.m.	7	7	7
10 a.m.	6	5	5
12 p.m.	3	3	3
2 p.m.	5	6	5
4 p.m.	3	4	4
6 p.m.	3	3	3
8 p.m.	4	1	2
10 p.m.	2	1	1

Once you've completed this record of your energy level, look for patterns. What time of day are you at your best?

Kyra, for example, a married mother of three, has the following energy chart:

You see from Kyra's numbers that midday and late afternoon are low energy times for her. She says, "I'm just dragging by lunch-time. I start to feel hungry by 11, but I can't break then. It's always a struggle to keep going until lunch."

Her husband, Paul's chart is very different. Paul changed the times in his chart to better reflect his work schedule (see Paul's chart on the next page).

Paul obviously is a night person. His energy is at its lowest in the early morning and late at night, but he goes strong through the late afternoons and evenings. Both Kyra and Paul have 4–6 hours during the day when they feel at the top of their game, and both admit that they'd love to feel that energized for a few more hours a day.

They can. It's as simple as a couple of small changes in what and when they eat.

Kyra is an early riser. By the time she's had a piece of toast and a cup of coffee, she's fully alert and ready for her day at the office.

Paul's Chart

	Day 1	Day 2	Day 3
9 a.m.	3	2	2
11 a.m.	3	3	3
1 p.m.	4	4	4
3 p.m.	5	6	5
5 p.m.	7	6	7
7 p.m.	7	7	7
9 p.m.	7	6	7
12 a.m.	3	3	3
2 a.m.	2	1	1

But, by 10 a.m. she notices a slump. She's looking for another cup of coffee to get her to lunchtime and if someone has brought in cookies or cake, she has a few bites to tide her over. Lunch revives Kyra and she feels good until after 2, when what she calls "the mid-afternoon slide" begins. Anticipating this drop in her mental energy, Kyra tries to complete the most demanding work in the morning and save the more routine tasks for late afternoon. An afternoon soda and a snack—usually something sweet or salty—keep her going until dinner. "I'm no good after that. I'm definitely a morning person. I spend my evenings with the kids since Paul has to work. If I have work to do, I get up early and do it before the kids get going. That works better for me."

Not so for her husband, Paul. His profile reveals what he knows about himself: mornings are not his best time. He's a night owl. "I hate it when I have to get up before 8, and I don't begin to really feel like myself until noon."

This is obvious from his chart. Paul's best time of day is late afternoon and evening. "That's when I do my best work." To keep himself going until then, Paul relies on Coca-Cola. "A couple of tall cokes and I'm good to go!" he says.

Until he crashes.

Paul admits that his day is a bit like a roller coaster. It takes quite a bit of soda to keep him riding high at his fast-paced, demanding job.

Everyone is wired by their own biology to follow certain daily rhythms. You shouldn't try to change them, but rather, work with them to extend your limits. Kyra, for instance, could effectively eliminate her mid-morning slump and much of her afternoon slide. If she added an ounce of protein at breakfast and a protein snack in the mid-afternoon, she could have a steady energy supply from morning to at least 4 p.m.

And Paul, although he will probably never be a morning person, doesn't have to wait until 4 in the afternoon to do his best work. Cutting back on the caffeine and sugar would eliminate some of the peaks and valleys he encounters in his day, and eating small protein snacks every few hours would give him more hours of strong performance.

Now, what about your children? Do you know what their energy levels are like throughout the day? You may not, though you could probably guess. If you're unsure, ask their teachers.

Teachers tell us that with few exceptions, kids tend to lose steam around mid-morning. Some kids arrive that way—they're the night owl kids. Unfortunately, school still doesn't accommodate younger children whose bodies' natural rhythms are better suited for a late start. Many children, though, are alert and ready at 8 to get to work. They can concentrate and focus. For about 2 hours.

Then the wiggles set in and the nods begin. Kids get restless. Their minds wander. They slump in their chairs and put their heads on their desk. They're hungry! They've run out of steam. If they're able, they'll go to a vending machine and grab a sugared drink, or some candy or a cookie. Anything to pick them up and give them a lift until lunch. They're pushed and prodded, coaxed and coached to lunchtime, when most kids make a mad tear for the lunchroom or to local fast food joints.

Helping your children figure out what keeps them in the zone for a great performance has different challenges at each stage of development. When your children are small, you have more control over what they eat, but they're less aware of their own mood states. Older children have greater capacity to be aware of and regulate their own mood states, but they want more control over what they consume. You can invite your kids to conduct their own experiments in which they discover for themselves the benefits of eating a little protein in the morning. For instance, encourage your kids to complete a log of their energy levels throughout the day for 5 days. Do this as a family and you're more likely to get their full cooperation. Help them to see the results by summarizing the patterns they observed as a graph or a few lines of description. What do they notice? Help them record what they observed. This information will serve as their baseline.

Then invite them to identify one small change they'd like to make for a week to see whether they can increase or extend their energy during the day. Start with the easy stuff—small changes that can result in big improvements in their ability to handle stress and anxiety.

For instance, if they don't already eat some protein with their breakfast every morning, begin there. Suggest some choices they can make that will get them 10–15 grams of protein. If they'll eat eggs, you could hard boil six at a time and keep them in the fridge where they're easy to grab. If they're picky eaters, you can show them how to make a shake in a blender with a cup of milk, a banana or berries, and a cup of yogurt, tofu, or two tablespoons of protein powder.

Table 1

Approximate Protein Content of Sample Foods

Food Item	Grams of Protein
Two eggs	12
8 oz of milk	9
1 oz cheese	7–9
⅓ cup cottage cheese	9
¼ cup peanut butter (4 Tbsp)	16
½ cup of nuts	16–25
3 oz tofu (a 1-inch slice)	4
3 oz meat (size of palm of your hand)	12–15
1 cup of yogurt	11
1 cup of beans	15

Use Table 1 for ideas on easy ways to eat small amounts of protein. I've included ideas for every kind of eater.

If your children already get enough protein in the morning, or if it's the mid-afternoon when they find themselves losing steam, they may want to try adding or substituting a small protein snack like peanut butter and crackers, a handful of almonds, or a cheese stick, instead of the cola or coffee and cookies they consume.

The more stress your children are under, the better their diet needs to be. You've heard this before but now may be the time to take a step toward doing something about it.

In addition to making sure they eat at least 10 grams of protein in the morning, there are three other changes your children can take to maintain strong levels of energy, focus, and concentration:

- reduce caffeine,
- reduce sugar, and
- sleep 8 hours each night.

PRACTICAL HELP

Protein bars are an easy and portable way to get 10–15 grams of protein at breakfast or breaks, and their cost is reasonable when you buy them by the box. But, beware protein bars that really are candy bars in disguise! Always check the labels for simple carbohydrates, sugars, and protein. As a general rule of thumb, anything with more than 25 grams of carbohydrate really is a candy bar pretending to be good for you. Look for bars that are 25 grams or less of carbohydrate, less than 10 grams of sugar, and at least 10 grams of protein. Anything below 15 grams of carbohydrates probably will not taste good enough to eat. Some of the popular "high energy" or "health food" bars have a whopping 40+ grams of carbohydrates and nearly 300 calories!

Reduce Caffeine and Sugar

With the popularization of several national chains, many children have taken up the coffee habit. As a result, younger and younger children are consuming large amounts of caffeine. Although caffeine increases their capacity to do work, it also can take them out of their zone of optimal performance. Children who struggle with high levels of anxiety in particular often are sensitive to even very small levels of caffeine and need to cut it way back. How do you know how much is too much?

The U.S. government has no guidelines about children's caffeine consumption, but the Canadian government recommends the following daily limits:

- 45 mg for 4- to 6-year-olds,
- 62.5 mg for 7- to 9-year-olds, and
- 85 mg for 10- to 12-year-olds.

Table 2

Caffeine Content in Various Beverages and Foods

Product	Serving Size	Caffeine (mg)
Starbucks coffee	12 oz (350 ml)	375
Coke	12 oz (350 ml)	47
Mountain Dew	12 oz (350 ml)	56
Hot Chocolate	12 oz (350 ml)	25
Red Bull Energy Drink	8 oz (236 ml)	70
Black Tea, 5 minute brew	8 oz (236 ml)	46
Green Tea	8 oz (236 ml)	15
Dr. Pepper	12 oz (236 ml)	55
7 Up	12 oz (236 ml)	0
Chocolate candy bar	1 bar	25
M&M's	¼ cup (99 ml)	8
Starbucks Coffee Java Chip Ice Cream	½ cup (118 ml)	28
Dannon Coffee Yogurt	8 oz (236 ml)	45
Excedrin	2 tablets	130
No Doz	2 tablets	200

The chart in Table 2 lists the caffeine content in some common products. Note that persons who down several 100 mgs of caffeine a day may experience withdrawal symptoms when they cut back. Withdrawal symptoms include headaches, depression, and fatigue. Substituting decaffeinated products gradually in place of caffeinated drinks initially will make the weaning process easier for those who have a heavy caffeine habit.

Pediatrician Ann Engelland shares the concerns she has about kids and caffeine on *The Larchmont Gazette* Web site (available at http://www.larchmontgazette.com/2006/teenhealth) She says:

> As a frontline pediatrician, what are my concerns about caffeine and your kids?
>
> That kids are drinking coffee instead of eating healthy meals. That kids are too jazzed by the end of the day to wind down, spend some time relaxing and get enough sleep. That athletes use the "charge" of high caffeine drinks to energize their game, increasing the risk of injury and violent play. That kids begin a habit of using extraneous chemicals (i.e. caffeine) to fuel a life style that is too fast paced, stressful and unhealthy. That kids begin to mix their drugs in order to experiment with the pharmacology. About half of my patients do not eat breakfast.
>
> Too many girls are using caffeine as a diet pill and too many guys are using it as a pre-sports energizer. A granola bar in both cases would do a better job. Caffeine contributes to and enables the supercharged, over-scheduled lives you are teaching your kids to lead. Caffeine enables multi-tasking and in the short run it will lower your sleep requirements. But you forget that teenagers need time to daydream and relax and plenty of sleep for their *brain development*. What concerns me most is the notion that you need chemicals to bring us up, then different ones to bring us back down, then yet something else to put us somewhere right in between. You lose track of what feeling clean and natural can be like. (Engelland, 2006, ¶ 9–15).

How does caffeine rev up your children? It works by blocking adenosine, a chemical in the brain that slows its activity. Caffeine increases your children's levels of norepinephrine and adrenaline in the same way that stress does. These chemicals increase the reactivity of the nervous system, leaving children feeling wired and tense. It takes 30–60 minutes after drinking a cup of coffee for the caffeine to reach its peak concentration in a child's system and another 4–6 hours before the effects have worn off.

Psychologist Edward Bourne recommends that everyone keep their caffeine intake to less than 100 milligrams a day to manage their stress well, but there is tremendous range in individual differences in tolerance for caffeine, so it's up to you to decide what's best for you and your children. Some people feel irritable and nervous on as little as 200 mg. Dr. Engelland recommends that you limit children's caffeine intake to 300 mg a day at most. Whatever you decide, know that you can reduce your child's vulnerability to stress and anxiety by taking steps to limit his or her caffeine intake.

In addition to eating more protein and reducing caffeine, reducing sugar also will usually enhance performance. The average American eats more than 125 pounds of sugar a year. This is a 30% increase from just 20 years ago. It's too much. There is strong evidence that high levels of sugar consumption are associated with depression, anxiety, and difficulty handling stress.

Sugar, like caffeine, is a mood destabilizer. Increased levels of blood sugar trigger release of insulin, the hormone that stores the excess sugar as fat. As insulin goes to work converting sugar to fat, blood sugar levels drop. When blood sugar levels get low, the body feels tired and worn out (that's the crash many children and adults feel around 10 or 10:30 a.m.).

Sleep and Your Children's Brains

Are your children among the perpetually underrested? As many as 85% of adolescents and 71% of adults do not get enough sleep.

Performance, especially the ability to pay attention, focus, and respond efficiently, is related to sleep. Elite performers know this. They are religious about rest and recovery. What's the connection? Recent research on sleep suggests that sleep helps the brain:

- repair itself from the damage of daily stress;
- create new nerve cells; and
- improve memory, especially procedural memory.

Dr. K. A. Ericsson (2002), a researcher on high performance, notes that elite performers make rest a part of their routine. Surprisingly, most sleep about a full 8 hours and often take a short afternoon nap. World-class performers know that rest and recovery are essential to maintaining consistently outstanding performance. For them, rest is a discipline.

Sleep researchers are discovering that one reason you sleep may be because your brain needs to rest and repair itself. In fact, sleep may be more important for resting the mind than it is for resting the body. Every day, stress damages your brain, and every night, sleep helps your brain reduce the damage done by daily stress. One of the ways this seems to work is by maintaining adequate levels of an enzyme that is essential for repairing the damage caused by oxidative stress. Your muscles can rest any time you are still, but the only time your brain really rests is when you sleep. If your children don't get enough sleep, their brains don't get enough rest and the damage done by daily stress remains.

Sleep also may actually help the brain create new nerve cells. Scientists used to think that you were born with all of the nerve cells you were ever going to have, but now they know that the brain grows new cells, particularly in a part of the brain called the *dentate gyrus*. Recent studies suggest that not getting enough sleep inhibits the growth of new cells. In other words, there seems to be a *direct connection* between sleep and structural change in your brain.

Several researchers also believe that sleep plays an important role in securing memory. Robert Stickgold (2005), for instance, a professor of psychiatry at Harvard Medical School, found that sleep-deprived students do not remember new skills they've learned as well as students who get enough sleep. Memory studies from the last 10 years have demonstrated a benefit of sleep for memory.

Dr. Stickgold compares your child's need for sleep to her need for food but says that one difference is that most Americans will accept sleep starvation. Most people have been so sleep deprived for so long that they simply don't notice the difference. Sleep scientists will argue that most people's brains function most efficiently when they get a good 8 hours of sleep a day.

Evidence for sleep's benefit for what's called *procedural memory* is much stronger than for what's called *declarative memory*. Declarative memory is memory of facts, like dates of historical events, and procedural memory is memory for motor or perceptual skills like driving a car or playing a sport. Sleep researchers conclude that late night cramming may be justified for some kinds of tests, but not for others. If your child just has to regurgitate facts, it might be worthwhile to lose some sleep in order to memorize them, but if she's going to have synthesize some big ideas and write an essay under time pressure, she may be better off getting more sleep. Share this information with your teenagers.

There do seem to be ways to make up for lost sleep when your children are sleep deprived. Taking a 30–60 minute nap between noon and 3 p.m., and avoiding oversleeping on the weekends seem to help. In addition, many people find they can get more sleep if they follow these suggestions from sleep researchers:

- Avoid late night snacks—digestion prevents good rest.
- Don't oversleep on weekends; it can disrupt your natural sleep rhythms.
- Turn off the TV an hour before sleeping. Reducing stimulation helps your brain to relax.

Setting the Mood With Music

What else can you do to help your children manage their energy exchange efficiently? All of us know from experience that music can change your mood. In fact, "setting the mood" with music is commonplace when you plan an event. At a sporting event, rousing music is played during the team's warm-up, during breaks in play, and even during certain plays in the game. The same spirited music is played over and over to keep the crowd energized, which in turn energizes and motivates the team.

Some of us have hard, pulsing rock music in our iPod because it motivates us as we work out. Others of us have a CD of our favorite classical pieces to play as backdrop at work because it helps us to focus.

Music alters your mood. That's why the soundtrack for a movie can be as important as the visuals. The music sets the mood for the scene.

Help your children experiment with different music to explore the effects on their moods. Encourage them to listen to some music they haven't tried before and notice what effect, if any, it has. The worksheet on page 114 should help you and your kids pinpoint what music affects their moods.

Once your children know what music has the effect they want, they should listen to it enough so that they can play it in their head. That way, they can imagine it whenever they want to call on it to help manage their mood. Some people are more affected by music than others, so you'll have to experiment until your children know what kind of effect music has on their moods and then use it to their advantage.

Summary

Research on achievers points to the potential role that mood management may play in the development of talent. Elite achievers often are religious about their diet. They know that in order to give their best, they have to pay attention to what they eat. This is because what you eat can stress you out. Or, put you to sleep. Everyone has limits, but these can be extended. Mood management is about controlling the exchange of energy. A few basic habits can easily expand the limits of your children's energy and concentration. Eating some protein in the morning, substituting a small protein snack for the sweets children typically consume in the afternoon, reducing caffeine and making rest a part of their daily routine will increase the odds that they give a consistently great performance every day.

Mood Music

Ask your kids the following questions and record their answers below to determine what music affects their moods.

What music energizes you?

_____

_____

_____

What music calms you and helps you relax?

_____

_____

_____

What music makes you smile?

_____

_____

_____

What music makes you feel sad or irritable?

_____

_____

_____

Chapter Resources

Bourne, E., & Garano, L. (2003). *Coping with anxiety: 10 simple ways to relieve anxiety, fear & worry.* Oakland, CA: New Harbinger Publications.

Engelland, A. (2006, November 21). Getting the buzz on caffeine. *The Larchmont Gazette,* ¶ 9–15. Retrieved January 29, 2008, from http://www.larchmontgazette.com/2006/teenhealth

Ericsson, K. A. (2002). Attaining excellence through deliberate practice: Insights from the study of expert performance. In M. Ferrari (Ed.), *The pursuit of excellence through education* (pp. 21–56). London: Lawrence Erlbaum.

Kluger, J. (2006, January 16). The surprising power of the aging brain. *Time,* 84–87.

Ross, J. (2002). *Mood cure.* New York: Penguin Books.

Song, S. (2006, January 16). Sleeping your way to the top. *Time,* 83.

Stickgold, R. (2005). Sleep-dependent memory consolidation. *Nature, 437,* 1272–1278.

—7—

Learning Hope and Optimism

Winners work harder.

—anonymous

SUCCESS requires endurance. Whatever your children want to pursue, they have to learn how to keep at it. How do you keep your children motivated to work hard when they're faced with challenging work?

Motivation is tied to how children think. Specifically, it's tied to what they say to themselves about their success and failure experiences. How children interpret events is called their *explanatory style* and contributes to their sense of helplessness or empowerment. A hallmark of children who persevere through challenging circumstances is a positive explanatory style or *optimism*. We're not talking about an empty, pie in the sky kind of optimism, but a hopeful outlook that's grounded in reality. It's a perspective that keeps hope and motivation high.

Optimism can be learned. There are steps you can take today to develop your children's optimism so that they'll bounce back

 DOI: 10.4324/9781003237068-7

easily from setbacks and continue to strive when success does not come easily. You can promote your child's strong performance by teaching her to think positively about the day-to-day events in her life. In this chapter we'll look at the three dimensions of explanatory style and explore several strategies for developing your child's optimism.

Begin With Yourself

The first step is to take a look at what you're modeling. Your children are learning every day from your example. What are you teaching them? There are two ways you can measure your own optimism. One is with paper and pencil. The other is online.

If you prefer to take a paper-and-pencil questionnaire, you can borrow the book, *Learned Optimism* by Martin Seligman from your public library. The questionnaire and directions for scoring it are in Chapter 3 of Seligman's book.

If you have access to the Internet, a measure of your own optimism is only a few minutes away. Go to http://www.authentichappiness. org and click on Optimism Test. You'll need to register, but registration is free and will allow you to return to the site later and learn more. Complete the optimism questionnaire as directed online and submit your results. You'll immediately get several scores back. I suggest that you take the test and score your own explanatory style before reading on in this chapter. The description that follows will help you make sense of your scores.

Dimensions of Explanatory Style

Explanatory styles are categorized as optimistic or pessimistic and your child's style falls somewhere on the continuum from one to the other. Pessimistic children tend to be less resilient, more depressed, and achieve less in their lifetimes than optimistic children. Therefore, for children to realize their highest potential requires shaping and maintaining an optimistic style of interpreting success and failure experiences. You can support your child's strongest performance by teaching him or her to think positively about day-to-day events in his or her life.

Explanatory style has three dimensions: permanence, pervasiveness, and personalization. Each dimension has to do with how children think about the causes of positive and negative events.

Permanence, for instance, refers to whether a child sees the causes of events as temporary or enduring forever. When children believe that the causes of bad things will never change, their motivation decreases abruptly and discouragement sets in. Why keep trying if things aren't going to change? When they are disappointed, pessimists tend to think in terms of *always* and *never,* such as:

- I'll never get to . . .
- It's always going to . . .
- My friends will never . . .

It's easy to understand how children who think this way end up feeling hopeless and apathetic.

Optimists, on the other hand, view setbacks as temporary. They think in terms of *sometimes* and *recently.* When they experience disappointments, they say to themselves things like:

- I've been really stressed lately . . .
- Sometimes school is difficult . . .
- She's been in a bad mood recently . . .

Optimistic children are more likely to persevere in the face of adversity because they feel hopeful that things will change. They see the causes of disappointments as time limited, so they remain encouraged and energized.

When things go well, optimists believe the causes of success are permanent, while pessimists believe the causes are temporary. When they succeed, optimists say things to themselves like:

- I did well on that paper because I am good with words, or I've always been a good writer.
- I'm a natural athlete.

Pessimists, on the other hand, say things like,

- I won't be able to keep this up.
- I'm not usually this well-prepared.
- I had a good day.

Because of this difference in how they explain their achievements, success builds confidence for kids with a positive explanatory style, but has little impact on the confidence or self-esteem of kids whose style is negative.

Here's a summary of what we've covered so far:

When They Fail . . .

Optimists	**Pessimists**
Think of it as temporary.	Think of it as permanent.
I'll do better next time.	*This is never going to end.*

When They Succeed . . .

Optimists	**Pessimists**
Think of it as permanent.	Think of it as temporary.
I'm going to win the state meet.	*I won't be able to repeat this.*

The second dimension of explanatory style is *pervasiveness*. It refers to projecting causes across many different situations.

Pessimists tend to generalize the causes of bad events, while optimists tend to limit the effects. As a result, when things don't go well, optimists compartmentalize their problems more easily and move on with their lives. They say things like,

- I don't like the way Ms. Ankeny graded on this test.
- The director is upset about how that scene went.
- We lost that round, but we'll get the next one.

They remain engaged with difficult tasks, even when they don't like what's happening.

Pessimists, on the other hand, tend to catastrophize and see their entire world unraveling when one bad event occurs. They generalize from one setback to other children or events and say things like:

- Teachers are unfair.
- Coach has it in for the defense.
- You can never please a director.

As a result, they quickly feel hopeless about their circumstances and give up.

When they're successful, pessimists and optimists do the reverse. Pessimists localize the causes and optimists generalize them. For instance, an optimistic child who does well on a math test may say to herself:

- I'm a good student.
- I do well on tests.

Do you see how such thinking builds her confidence? She generalizes from a specific success to broader triumphs. In contrast, the pessimistic child who does just as well limits the effects of her success, saying something like:

- I'm good at shooting, but I can't dribble or pass the ball.
- I got a good grade on that paper because I liked the subject.
- I can do fractions, but I'm terrible at word problems.

Do you see how such thinking constrains her?

Kids who limit the effects of negative events and generalize the effects of positive events are less likely to lose their motivation, and are more likely to persevere when they face challenges. Here's a summary:

When They Fail . . .

Optimists	**Pessimists**
Limit the effect.	Generalize.
I had a bad day.	*My whole life stinks.*

When They Succeed . . .

Optimists	**Pessimists**
Generalize.	Limit the effect.
My life is getting better all the time.	*This is the only class where I do well.*

The third dimension of explanatory style is *personalization* and it refers to a child's beliefs about who or what is responsible for events. Your children believe that either they're responsible for their success or failure, or they believe that external circumstances contributed.

Pessimists blame themselves when things go badly and fail to take enough credit when things go well. Optimists do the reverse, taking credit for their successes and acknowledging the role of outside factors when outcomes are disappointing. Some children are so hard on themselves when they fail to hit the mark that they have a very hard time recovering from upsets. The attacks they make on their own character keep them from trying again and from being able to examine their mistakes. What you're aiming for is to develop your child's ability to look at his or her achievements realistically and accurately.

Optimistic kids are not children who don't hold themselves accountable and accept responsibility for their errors. Rather, when disappointments are the result of some weakness of theirs, they acknowledge their need to address those specific deficits without disparaging their entire character. They differentiate between their behavior and their character.

How do you feel if you think that problems are always all your fault? What happens to your self-confidence and general outlook over time if you rarely pat yourself on the back for your successes? It's easy to understand how such thinking makes kids want to give up. Here's a summary of what we've said so far about personalization:

When They Fail . . .

Optimists	**Pessimists**
Consider outside factors.	Blame themselves.
I was up late.	*I'm a jerk.*

When They Succeed . . .

Optimists	**Pessimists**
Take credit.	Give credit to external factors.
I've worked hard.	*The judges were easy.*

Now let's look at an illustration that demonstrates how these differences might play out in real life.

REAL LIFE

Marcus and Nikki both participated in their school district's music festival. Marcus played piano and Nikki played violin. Marcus took first place, while Nikki didn't place at all. Surprisingly, Marcus didn't seem as pleased with his performance as Nikki was, even though he did better. The difference in their reactions is related to their explanatory styles. Marcus tends to be more pessimistic while Nikki is more optimistic. Even though he did very well, Marcus attributes his success to temporary circumstances. "Some of the other kids actually play better than I do but they had a bad day. I heard that one of the guys wasn't feeling well and this girl I know must have had an off day because she's usually very good." Marcus believes he won by default.

Nikki, on the other hand, gives an optimistic explanation for her mediocre finish. She says, "I didn't place because I made too many errors, but my interpretation was better and I did really well remembering the music. If I practice more, I'll place next time." Nikki attributes her performance to something that is highly changeable—the time she devotes to practice. Plus, she affirms qualities in herself that are enduring—her musicality and her memory.

Over time, Nikki is likely to gain more ground than Marcus, even though Marcus technically may be the better musician, because her optimism will keep her working hard and striving to do better, while Marcus' pessimism will keep him feeling deflated about his accomplishments.

Now let's consider two talented children, each with a different explanatory style. Davion is a gifted 14-year-old who enjoys soccer and hanging out with his friends. He recently earned strong marks on a national test and has consistently earned good grades, with the exception of social studies, where he earns only mediocre grades. Even though he does well, Davion's parents and teachers are concerned about him because he doesn't put forth much effort. He always seems to want to slide by doing as little as possible, and when confronted with a challenge, he tends to look for shortcuts or an easy exit.

Davion was enthusiastic about school and soccer when he was in elementary school, but his parents note that his motivation has really waned since he hit adolescence. He has elected not to take some of the advanced classes his school offers and doesn't embrace challenge in any other arena either. In spite of his long history of relative "success" in school, Davion doesn't see himself as particularly intelligent or competent. He seems to be losing confidence as he gets older and is negative more often about his friendships and his future.

A number of things might explain Davion's behavior, but one strong possibility is his explanatory style. Even though he has done well academically and socially over the years, Davion may be quite pessimistic, believing his successes are due to external factors that are temporary and easily lost. When he does well, he may say to himself things like:

- The teachers at my school are easy graders.
- The work isn't very difficult.
- The coach likes me.

If Davion's explanatory style is largely pessimistic, then he may believe that the positive experiences in his life are not likely to last, and he may fail to give himself enough credit for the strong social and academic skills he does possess. If so, he'll have trouble when he confronts real adversity for the first time. In the face of adversity, pessimists make discouraging statements to themselves that increase their desire to give up.

Ti, on the other hand, is an ambitious fifth grader who also has several good friends and enjoys school. She has a mild learning disability and ADHD, but in spite of these obstacles, she does well in school and has strong self-esteem. Ti is deeply curious about a great many things, and will spend long hours learning what she can about animals, her passion. Ti has to work harder than many of her classmates to get similar results, and has a particularly tough time in testing situations, but she is learning to cope and is developing a sense of humor about her limitations.

Again, there are probably several factors contributing to Ti's emotional health, social competence, and academic confidence. One likely factor is that she has an optimistic explanatory style. Ti probably takes credit for her successes, saying things to herself like, "Other kids like me because I'm funny," and "I do better in school when I remember to take my medication and study for a test."

When she experiences minor setbacks, Ti probably does not berate herself or others, but says things to herself like, "My friends got upset because I was interrupting," and "I got a B because I lost my notes from the film we watched."

Because she doesn't generalize the causes of her failure experiences, nor personalize them, Ti remains engaged in the struggle when she faces challenge and feels confident. She remains hopeful and believes things will improve if she continues to work hard. She feels encouraged.

Even though Davion has had an easier time with schoolwork and making friends than Ti, he may be more at risk for withdrawal, discouragement, and poor motivation because he is the more pessimistic thinker.

The Link Between Pessimism and Discouragement

Pessimism and discouragement form a vicious circle. Pessimism causes discouragement and discouragement creates a more negative view of life. Viewing life more negatively exacerbates discouragement, which leads to depression. The more discouraged your children get, the harder it becomes for them to make an effort. Then, avoidance and procrastination set in, and trying to motivate them feels like moving a mountain. Pessimists become passive when faced with adversity. At a time when more effort is called for, they exert less. More disappointments follow, deepening their discouragement. When you're discouraged, setbacks and rejections are harder to take. Quitting begins to look attractive. Once children begin fantasizing about quitting, it's nearly impossible to turn them around.

Becoming More Positive

It's easy to coach your child to greater optimism. Just
- talk,
- listen, and
- teach.

We've already talked about the first one—watch what you say. Make sure you're modeling optimism. Affirm your child with permanent and pervasive messages when she's succeeding, not when she struggles or misbehaves. Say:
- You'll have to practice more if you want to win.
- Your memory is getting better and better.

- You acted without thinking; next time stop and consider the consequences.
- You play like a champion.
- You struggled because you lost your concentration.

Second, listen to your children when they are talking about their successes and their disappointments. What are they saying to themselves? To what do they attribute their victories and defeats? How constructive or destructive are their explanations for their successes and failures? Most of us intuitively recognize the dangers of negative thinking when things go badly, but you probably didn't realize that how your children think about their success is just as vital. Listen closely to what they say. The worksheet on the next page provides a good exercise in listening closely.

If you want a clearer picture of your children's optimism, you can assess it as you did your own with the children's questionnaire you'll find in Martin Seligman's book, *The Optimistic Child*. You can find this great book in the parenting section of any major bookstore or your public library and copy the questionnaire to give to your children. Or, take some paper and a pencil to your favorite bookstore, and let your child take the quiz while you get some coffee. You'll have to score it for him.

You'll get at least seven scores for your child. You'll find out how optimistic or pessimistic he is on each of the three dimensions for success and for failure experiences and you'll get a general hope score that lets you know how hopeful your child is. Once you're familiar with the way your child tends to think about pleasing and unsatisfying outcomes, you're ready to help him or her become more optimistic. In addition to the questionnaire, Seligman's book is chock full of practical, easy-to-follow ideas about how you can promote optimism in your children at home.

What They Really Say

Try this exercise. "Listen" to the explanations given in each of the scenarios below and decide whether they're optimistic or pessimistic. Try to determine what dimensions are reflected in the explanations. I've done the first one for you. The answers are included in the answer key at the back of this book (see pp. 175–176).

Dion is selected for a competitive summer arts camp. He says, "All of that work I put into my audition tape really paid off."

Optimistic or Pessimistic? <u>Optimistic.</u>
What dimensions are reflected here? <u>Personalization—he takes credit for his success.</u>

Now you do the rest on your own and check your answers at the end of the book.

1. Maryah doesn't make her community's top soccer team. She says, "I did my best but I don't handle the ball as well as those who made the team. I'll go to soccer camp this summer and improve."

Optimistic or Pessimistic? _____

What dimensions are reflected here? _____

_____

2. Nora is popular at her new school. She says, "They like me because I'm Xavier's friend."

Optimistic or Pessimistic? _____

What dimensions are reflected here? _____

_____

3. Lucas does so well on a national standardized test he's awarded $1,000 scholarship. He says, "I didn't study. I just guessed. "

Optimistic or Pessimistic? _____

What dimensions are reflected here? _____

_____

4. Chloe does poorly at an audition. She says, "I got so nervous I couldn't breathe."

Optimistic or Pessimistic? _____

What dimensions are reflected here? _____

_____

5. Noah works hard on a short story and submits it to a magazine for publication. It's rejected. He says, "I can't write. I'll never get anything published."

Optimistic or Pessimistic? _____

What dimensions are reflected here? _____

_____

Practice with your children. The next time they do well or experience a disappointment, keep a sharp ear to their explanations. Listen for patterns. Do they pat themselves on the back when they do well? Are they limiting their success or generalizing it? When they're not happy with the job they've done, do they tend to think of the causes as permanent or temporary? Once you're familiar with your child's explanatory style, you're ready to begin shaping it to greater optimism.

Teach Them to Consider More Than One Explanation

It's not helpful to try to talk your children out of their way of thinking. Pep talks, compliments, and that-a-boys may make you and them feel better momentarily, but they're not likely to have much impact on how your children think about future challenges. Discouraged children often give up easily because they have trouble seeing more than one reason for failure and the reason usually is permanent and personal. They blame themselves for setbacks. You can teach them to consider a greater range of explanations.

In the example that follows, notice how Gavin's father gently questions him to help guide his thinking about the meaning of a failed audition.

Gavin's music teacher has encouraged him to try out for a community theater production because she thinks the experience will build his confidence and develop his talent but Gavin is reluctant. His father talks with him about his hesitation.

"I just don't want to," insists Gavin.

"But, you love to sing. Ms. Tong thinks you have a good chance of getting a part."

"Dad, I won't get a part. Lots of kids sing way better than I do."

"True, but most of them probably won't be trying out for this production and even if they do, so what? It will be good experience."

"Dad, I won't get selected."

"So? What would it mean to you if you didn't?"

"It means . . . I don't know what it means."

"Well, let's think about that for a minute. What are the possibilities?"

"It only means one thing."

"Oh? What's that?"

"I can't sing."

"Really? You think if you don't make this audition it means you don't have a good singing voice?"

"What else?"

"Gavin, when children audition, there are lots of reasons they don't get a part. It's not just about their talent. You've been to auditions before. What are some reasons children don't get a part?"

"Sometimes because they're not right for the part—it's their appearance or they're too tall or too short, or sometimes it's because there are other children who are better than they are—they don't perform their best on the day of audition maybe, or there's more competition."

"Exactly. What are some other reasons?"

Gavin shrugs, "Maybe their voice isn't right for the part, or they don't fit well with the other characters . . ."

"Auditions are very competitive, Gavin. The only way to get good at them is to audition a lot. If you want to sing on stage you need to develop your ability to audition well."

"Okay. I guess it can't hurt to try. Will you help me prepare? Ms. Tong said she would give me some music for the audition."

"Sure. Let's give it your best shot and we'll see what happens. If you get the part, great. If you don't get the part, we'll learn from the experience."

In the next example, see how it's possible to use even the everyday disappointments that arise with even young children to shape their explanatory style.

Six-year old Makayla is devastated because she didn't get invited to a classmate's birthday party. When she has stopped crying and had her dinner, her mother invites her to sit at the table with her where she has some crayons and a large piece of paper.

"Makayla, will you draw something with me? Choose a color and make as big a circle as you can on this piece of paper."

Makayla takes a purple crayon and carefully draws a very big circle.

"I like how big you made it," says her mother. "Now divide the circle in two parts. Draw a line straight across from one side all the way to the other."

As Makayla draws the line she asks, "What are we making?"

"We're making a great big pizza pie. Your favorite, with lots of pepperoni and extra cheese." When Makayla finishes the line her mother says "Let's cut the pizza into lots of pieces. How many pieces can you make?"

Makayla draws one line after another, occasionally choosing other colors, and as she draws her mother says, "Makayla, there are lots of reasons children don't get invited to a party. Can you tell me one reason?"

"Cause they don't like them."

"Yes, that can be one reason why children are not invited. There are other reasons, too. Can you think of one?"

"Cause they don't want them at the party?"

"Yes, that's another reason. You've thought of two. I can think of another reason."

"What is it?"

"Because her mother said she could only have eight children. Maybe she wanted to invite more of her friends but her mother said she could only have eight."

"Cause they were going to the zoo."

"Yes. Maybe the children are going somewhere in the car and there's only enough room for a few children. Let's think of other reasons why children don't get invited to a party. I'll write them inside the pizza pieces you draw."

Makayla has trouble coming up with another reason so her mother helps her by asking, "Remember your birthday party? You wanted to invite some people, but we didn't. What were the reasons?"

"It was a girl's party."

"That's right. Some parties are just for boys or just for girls. What's another reason? You wanted to invite Callie to your party, but you didn't. Remember? Why was that?"

"She has allergies."

"That's right. Callie can't come to our house because we have two cats. Cats make her sick. I'll write that reason in this piece right here. You've made a lot of pieces of pizza. You fill in the pepperoni and I'll write in the reasons some children don't get invited to parties. What's another reason?"

In just 10 minutes, Makayla and her mother come up with eight different reasons children are sometimes not invited to parties. Makayla may not remember this next time she is upset about a defeat, but with practice, she'll be less likely to consider only one explanation for events and develop the habit of looking outside herself for circumstances that contribute to disappointing outcomes.

Discussing Pessimism and Optimism

As you read to your children or watch movies together, talk about the characters' perspectives on success and failure. Adventure films and stories are great for this, as are stories based on true events. Discuss the reasons children persevered. What kept them going against the odds? How did they view their failures and setbacks? To what did they attribute their success?

Discuss with your children times when your thoughts or theirs were particularly optimistic or pessimistic. What was that like? What did they notice happened to their self-confidence? How much did they feel like working toward a solution? How easy is it to persevere in the pursuit of high goals if one is pessimistic? Emphasize the relationship between thoughts and feelings.

Coping With Setbacks

The road to higher levels of performance is not a straight uphill climb. It includes unexpected detours. The way in which we respond to these temporary defeats distinguishes those who continue on from those who do not.

Most achievers are familiar with slumps, those downward spirals of defeat and disappointment that seem to get worse the harder they try. Slumps seem to come upon us out of nowhere, but psychologists argue that they usually arise from a lack of adequate mental preparation for increased levels of stress and competition. Conditioning for any kind of high achievement is about training psychologically, as well as training academically, musically, or physically.

One factor contributing to slumps is unrealistic expectations of performance. Only the mediocre are at their best 100% of the time. If achievers expect to give their absolute best every time, then when results are not as they imagined, they may think they are not as good as they thought they were. This distorted perception can, in turn, subtly contribute to a change in their work habits and effort.

As an example, consider a child who has performed at the top of her class in science and has won some awards at science fairs. Then, there follows a season when she does not do as well as she used to. Her grades are still good, but she's not first in her class. If she begins to feel anxious about this, if she begins to think that she's not as good as she used to think she was, or fears that maybe children have been wrong about her, that she's not really as talented as they said, she could become more anxious when taking tests, or feel less confident when making a presentation. Her fearful reaction, in turn, puts her at a disadvantage.

To counter this, you must help your child understand the nature of peak performance. You must help her realize that some of her performances will be better than others. Working very hard for several weeks or months at anything typically results in a plateau, after which there is no perceived improvement for a while. If achievers respond to this change in progress with fear, their anxious thoughts can trigger a cascade of physiologic reactions that interfere with achievement. They need to learn to see such changes as a normal part of the talent development process and to take charge of their self-talk, that interior monologue they have with themselves. When positive, this self-talk will help them stay focused, but when negative, it can distract and derail them from the track of higher achievement.

Summary

As competition intensifies and stakes rise, perseverance makes the difference. Perseverance is a learned behavior that's fueled to a large degree by explanatory style—how children think about the reasons for their success or failures.

Children who stay motivated and remain positively engaged in the pursuit of high goals tend to attribute their success to their own effort and ability, while discouraged children tend to credit external factors. Motivated, optimistic children tend to generalize their success experiences, expecting that they will continue to do well and improve, while pessimistic children tend to limit the effects of their successes. When they have a setback, optimists do not generalize the negative effects, but limit them, telling themselves that the experience will improve with time, while pessimists generalize from one negative experience to other areas of their life. Explanatory style influences motivation, perseverance, and realistic risk-taking. It is not difficult to shape explanatory style, and we know that the positive effects of shaping explanatory style in school-aged children can last for years.

Chapter Resources

Greenberger, D., & Padesky, C. A. (1995). *Mind over mood: Change the way you feel by changing the way you think*. New York: Guilford Press.

Johnson, M. B., Enenbaum, G., & Edmonds, W. A. (2006). Adaptation to physically and emotionally demanding conditions: The role of deliberate practice. *High Ability Studies, 17*, 117–136.

McGinnis, A. (1990). *The power of optimism.* New York: Harper Collins.

Peterson, C., Maier, S., & Seligman, M. (1993). *Learned helplessness.* New York: Oxford.

Seligman, M. (1990). *Learned optimism.* New York: Random House.

Seligman, M. (1995). *The optimistic child.* New York: HarperCollins.

—8—

Reconciling the Need to Belong With the Need to Achieve

SUCCESS comes with a price. Tony knows this all too well. He is a gifted, Latino eighth grader with excellent test scores. His teachers and parents know he's capable of much better than the C's he earns in class. Although he actively participates in class discussions and seems genuinely interested in some of his subjects, he consistently fails to turn in homework or put forth much effort on tests. When asked about it, he just shrugs and says he'd rather be with his friends. His teachers worry that if he decides not to take the accelerated classes, he'll just coast and settle for mediocre grades.

Tony's parents are concerned about him too. They encourage him to do his work and have offered a variety of incentives and punishments during the past 2 years, but all he seems to want to do is listen to music with his friends.

Tony's parents emigrated to the U.S. when they were children, and they place a high value on education. Tony seems to want to have nothing to do with the hard work that contributed to his par-

 DOI: 10.4324/9781003237068-8

ents' success. What's going on? If Tony is so capable, why won't he agree to take the challenging courses?

As they get older, many talented children feel torn between their desire to do well and their desire to belong. For some children, this tension becomes so strong they will do almost anything to make it go away—even quit. Conflicts between the need to belong and the need to achieve are especially common among smart girls, minority children, children from humble homes, and creatively talented boys. These tensions can erode their aspirations and self-esteem.

Chenda, for instance, is a sixth grader who plays the clarinet, loves science, and has been conducting her own research with a physician mentor for 2 years. Halfway through this year, however, she suddenly lost interest in science and her mentorship. It seemed to happen overnight and shocked her parents.

> She used to be thrilled to see her mentor. It was the highlight of her week. And, she always raved about her science class, but lately she seems indifferent. What's going on?

Chenda is starting to realize that her achievement has social costs. Though little is said to her directly, she's becoming aware of the subtle and not so subtle messages about smart girls, girl scientists, and kids who love academics. In Chenda's peer group, there's a social price to pay for high motivation and achievement, so Chenda is pulling back, hesitant to pursue her goals and reluctant to abandon her peer group.

Daniel also is reluctant about the classes he wants to take, for similar reasons. His passion is theater and art, but in the middle school he attends in a southern rural community, the unspoken expectation is that boys his age should be excited about athletics. Although he doesn't mention it, Daniel understands that there's a limit to how much drama and art he can take before he, too, pays a price.

The issues that Tony, Chenda, and Daniel struggle with are common among high-ability children. Uncomfortable dissonance arises when the need to achieve conflicts with the need to belong. They sometimes find themselves the target of criticism, or ostracism, or feel unappreciated, rejected, or misunderstood. Over time, many of them lower their sights, abandon their passions, or give up on the most challenging work.

This happens because the world doesn't always appreciate talent and it often gives mixed messages to kids who are on the road to high performance. If you have a smart, talented daughter, she may hear messages like:

- Compete but be nice.
- Be ambitious, but don't act like a man.
- Be smart, but not too smart.
- Be the best, but be popular (and sexy).

Your daughter may feel torn between high achievement and social acceptance.

Or, you may have an artistically gifted son who is sensitive to messages like these:

- Express yourself, but don't cry.
- Do your best, but don't act gay.
- Real men like sports.

Talented kids from different ethnic and racial groups also hear mixed messages about their pursuit of higher achievement from the media, their peers, and even from well-meaning family members:

- Achieve, but don't act White.
- Do well, but don't think too much of yourself.
- Work hard, but take care of others first.

In some cultures, high achievement is looked upon with distrust, suspicion, or even contempt. Upward mobility may be viewed as a betrayal or rejection. Parents who value a steady paycheck now more than the distant possibilities of college education might actively discourage their children from the pursuit of higher achievement, saying things like:

- You can take that advanced course provided you can still help out after school.
- What do you need to go to college for?
- Have you become too good for us now?
- We can't afford lessons. You should know better than to ask.

Let's pause here for a moment and give you a chance to reflect on your own experience with the price of success. What has achieving your goals cost you?

_____

_____

_____

_____

The essence of keeping motivation and achievement high is not so much avoiding these conflicts, but developing the attitudes and skills needed to manage them as they arise. Your job as a parent is to anticipate these conflicts and provide some direct coaching in specific coping strategies. Certain kinds of supports will keep conflicts between the need to belong and the need to achieve from undermining your children's motivation and achievement. Let's look at where you can start.

Talk About It

The first step is to talk about it. Shared dialogue with your children has a liberating power that seems to give children permission to stay the course of high achievement. Frank discussions about the following realities will help your child grow more confident in his or her ability to manage the conflicts that will arise:

- The circles we move in don't always appreciate talent.
- Some friends or family members aren't going to be happy about your success.
- The more you achieve, the greater the social costs may be.

An easy way to get the conversation going with your children is to watch movies together that depict talented youth struggling to resolve their need to belong with their need to pursue their dreams. Some popular movies with this theme include:

- *Bend It Like Beckham*
- *Akeelah and the Bee*
- *October Sky*
- *Billy Elliott*
- *Finding Forrester*
- *Smoke Signals*
- *Little Man Tate*

For example, the feel-good movie, *Bend It Like Beckham,* tells the story of Jess, a teenage daughter of an East Indian Sikh living in London who has her heart set on becoming a soccer player. Jess knows that she has athletic talent and she loves the game, but her parents think her time would be better spent learning to cook and preparing herself for marriage. Her parents don't think it's appropriate for a girl her age to be dressed in shorts instead of the traditional salwar kameez. Jess has to decide how to cope with the conflicting expectations and desires in her life. The conflict comes to a crisis point when she has an opportunity to play in an important soccer tournament on the day of her sister's wedding.

October Sky is based on the true story of Homer Hickam, a coalminer's son who was inspired by Sputnik to pursue his passion for rocketry despite the fact that most people in his community believed he was wasting his time and did not support his desire to go to college. The movie realistically depicts the conflicts and tensions Homer had to persevere through in order to attend college and later become an aerospace engineer for NASA.

As you watch these or other movies with your children, talk about the challenges the main characters face and how they resolve them. Use the following starter questions as a guide or create your own:

- What are the obstacles this person has to overcome in order to pursue his or her dream?
- Which obstacle do you think is the biggest, or most difficult? Why?
- Who supports this person in his or her pursuit of a dream? In what ways do they show their support?
- Choose one or two people who stand in this person's way and explain what you think are the reasons that they do not support this person's goals. What kinds of messages do they give?
- Explain how the main character deals with the obstacles that he or she faces.
- What do you think of his or her strategy?
- What do you think will happen to this person's family relationships as he or she gets older?

Watching movies together is a good place to begin because it's less threatening and easier for many children to discuss an issue as it relates to someone else than it is to discuss how it relates to themselves. Older children, in particular, may be more willing to talk about the conflict they feel between their desire to achieve and their desire to belong after they've talked about those tensions as portrayed by a neutral character in a story or film.

Use Good Stories to Build Their Confidence

Like good movies, reading the personal accounts of high achievers who have found ways to cope with the tensions they feel because their talents or interests are not always valued can be useful too, as it gives children a chance to explore the issue from other perspectives.

Guided reading in good literature can help your children gain an understanding of themselves and others and can help them learn ways to cope with new or difficult situations. By identifying with the characters in great books, children vicariously experience roles, attitudes, or feelings they haven't experienced before, and gain new insights into

PRACTICAL HELP

Finding Forrester tells the tale of Jamal, an African American high school student, whose high score on a state exam and whose talent on the basketball court earns him a full scholarship to attend an elite high school in Manhattan. His family's support and his relationship with a reclusive Pulitzer Prize winner empower him to overcome racial prejudice and class bias to pursue his dream of writing.

Akeelah and the Bee is an upbeat, inspirational story about 11-year-old Akeelah, an African American girl from Los Angeles with a strong aptitude for words. With the support of several adults in her life, Akeelah overcomes her concern about what her classmates will think of her and enters several spelling contests, eventually earning herself a spot in the Scripps National Spelling Bee.

solutions to similar challenges in their own lives or into alternative coping strategies. The emotional distance provided by reading is less threatening to children than talking about their own lives directly, so they are more open to new ideas. It's easier to critically examine the conflict between the need to achieve and the need to belong in your own life if you've looked at in the life of someone else first.

There are a few guidelines you'll want to follow when using books as a strategy to teach your children coping skills. The first is to use high-quality literature. I've given you a few titles to consider in the sidebar on page 147, but you also can ask your child's teacher or a librarian to recommend award-winning children's stories or something similar. Because identification with the characters is essential for this strategy to work, you want the best literature—stories in which characters are well-developed and the storyline is engaging and appropriate for your child's age.

Select stories that support high achievement and hard work. Look for optimistic stories in which there are characters struggling through obstacles to make their dreams come true or to achieve something of value. Young children like to read stories over and over, while older children will want to move on to a new one. Keep in mind that many teenagers enjoy hearing a good story read aloud, even if it was intended for a younger person. Stories for younger children speak to the child in all of us.

Keep the focus of your discussion on the characters and on the problem in the story. You don't have to discuss every book that you and your children read together, but when you do, the goal is to get your children to reflect on the story, not for you to make a point or give a mini-lecture. Follow your child's lead. Listen a lot and speak little. If you're not sure how to get started, you can use the same discussion questions suggested earlier for movies.

Calculating the Costs of Success

Talk with your children about the costs of success. This isn't a one-time chat you have but an ongoing conversation. Ask them think to imagine how attaining one of their dreams might change their life. One thing always leads to another. For instance, how might their life change if they do gain admission to that competitive summer camp, enroll in a private school, publish a book, or make the best team?

Talk about what life might be like if they do become famous, earn a prestigious award, make a lot of money, or earn a great deal of status. They have much less privacy and less freedom to go where they want when they want. They might get to be in charge of something very exciting and have a lot of influence. They might have more responsibility and work longer and harder. Realizing our dreams always comes with a price.

Work with your children to make a map of all of the good and bad things that might happen if they were to realize their goals. What might they gain? What might they lose? The point is to realistically appraise the potential effects of their future success and to begin

PRACTICAL HELP

For younger children, books like Paul Fleischman's (1999) *Weslandia*, or Megan McDonald's (1995), *Insects Are My Life*, are engaging and provocative introductions to these issues. For older children, stories such as *Mama's Girl*, by Veronica Chambers (1997), *My Name Is Asher Lev* by Chaim Potok (1972), and *Rocket Boys* by Homer Hickam (2000), serve as realistic illustrations of the tensions gifted young people may experience when they are members of cultures that do not value certain behaviors associated with talent. These and true accounts like Ron Suskind's (1998) moving story about a gifted Black teenager's journey from the inner city to the Ivy League in *A Hope in the Unseen* may offer a foundation from which your children can begin to make sense of the contradictions and unfairness they experience in their own pursuits of excellence.

REAL LIFE

In an interview with National Public Radio, 17-year-old Todd Kramer, winner of one of the 2007 $50,000 Davidson Fellowships, had this to say about what his achievement in music has cost him:

A devotion to musical study has also caused me to make certain sacrifices. I have not had any free Saturdays during the academic year since third grade and have had less time to participate in non-musical activities. For example, going to Juilliard made continuing basketball and chess impossible at an age when those types of activities were very important to me. However, I can say that it was worth the sacrifice. I have had experiences in music that will last a lifetime. (From the Top, 2008, ¶ 1)

to think about how they can cope with these changes. People succeed every day and their lives are changed. Thousands of people have learned to manage the emotional and social costs of success, and thousands have quit because they couldn't. You want your child in the first group.

Take a big piece of newsprint or butcher paper and write one of your child's dreams in the middle of it (e.g., win an Olympic medal, be a race car driver, play in the symphony, raise horses, etc.). Then, working together, come up with one positive outcome of that success and one negative outcome.

For instance, Chenda's dream is to become a pediatrician. One positive outcome she sees right now is that she'll be able to help families. A negative is that she'll be in training a very long time.

Examine each outcome and ask your child to think of one positive and one negative result of it. Chenda says that one advantage of helping families is that her work will be very rewarding. She'll be admired and respected and have the satisfaction of knowing that she's made a difference in the lives of people. A disadvantage is that she'll work long hours and be on call. She'll have less time for her personal life.

The upside of being in training until age 30 is that she'll have the opportunity to make an excellent salary. The more specialized she is, the more money she'll make. The downside is that she'll have little time in her twenties for dating or romance. She may have to wait until after 30 to have children if she wants a family.

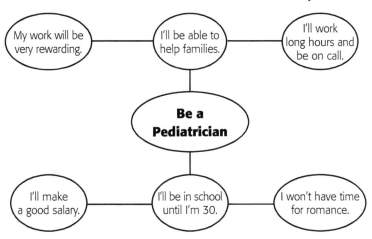

If you do a similar map with your children, don't stop at just two outcomes. Continue to map the potential benefits and costs of success until you run out of space on the paper. Now you have something to talk about.

Here's how Chenda's conversation might go with her mother:

Chenda: One bad thing is it might be lonely going to medical school.

Mother: True. Med students work very hard. They don't have much time for meeting with friends outside of school.

Chenda: I wouldn't want to live without friends.

Mother: I wouldn't want you to either. Everyone needs friends. You'll have friends among your classmates in med school, though.

Chenda: Yeah, my best friends will probably be my classmates.

Mother: That's usually what happens. We make friends with people who like some of the same things as we do.

If Chenda's parents have had similar challenges—a time when work or school called for long hours and little time for diversions—they can share what that experience was like with her and how they coped. Or, they can wonder aloud how medical students cope with the common experience of fatigue and sacrifice. They may even know people who have been through it and who might be willing to talk about how they managed through those tough years.

Teach Them to Cope

. . . I learned to slip back and forth between my black and white worlds, understanding that each possessed its own language and customs and structures of meaning . . .
—Barack Obama, Illinois Senator and 2008 U.S. Presidential Candidate

One of the results of having some measure of success is that your children will begin to move in new social spheres. They'll have to navigate unfamiliar social relationships and cross new boundaries. This means that in addition to frank discussions about the pressures of high achievement, you'll need to teach your child specific coping skills. You'll need to provide pointed assistance in social skills because acceptable codes of conduct vary across settings.

Many children, for example, will need pointed assistance in *code switching*, a process of deliberately changing behaviors to accommodate the expectations of an environment. Behaviors that often change with social context include:

- greeting people,
- addressing people in authority,
- expressing a different opinion,
- questioning people in authority,
- casual conversation,
- etiquette, and
- joking or expressions of humor.

For instance, a child may wear the latest style at school, but be required to dress conservatively in his singing group. If you live in an urban area, your child may adhere to the "street code" for behavior when he's out and about in his neighborhood, and use more widely accepted behaviors when he leaves the neighborhood for other opportunities.

Code switching can be taught many ways. One is to identify the ways that dress, speech, gestures, and behaviors communicate "success" and "respect" in different settings and then practice them. Travel is great for this, and even within a single city there are lots of opportunities to observe and try on different behaviors. Many of us have learned to adjust our vocabularies and expressions to the expectations of different social contexts. If you negotiate more than one group at a time in your professional or personal life, you code switch without even thinking. You modify your vocabulary or speech, choose topics of conversation selectively, and even vary your dress.

The challenge for your child is to make the switches effectively without feeling like she doesn't belong. Conversations with older children or successful adults who actively negotiate two or more groups on a daily basis can help your child tap into her own insights about class, race, identity, and achievement and to develop an awareness of additional coping strategies. You might consider inviting successful young adults who can talk about the ways in which they cross cultural or class boundaries every day to speak to your child's class or team. Developing specific coping strategies will help your child pursue her achievement goals without feeling like she's betraying the group she belongs to or that she's compromising her integrity.

How comfortable and willing is my child to cross cultural and class boundaries? This is a key question to ask yourself. The more experiences you can provide for your child to meet and talk with people from different backgrounds than his own, the easier it will become for him to make the adjustments he'll need to make as he attains higher and higher achievement. Knowledge about self, culture, and social contexts is essential for fulfilling potential. Anything you can do to help your child clarify his beliefs, identify his values, recognize explicit and implicit expectations from family and community, and describe traditions is valuable.

Who's On Your Team?

People who realize their dreams don't do it on their own. When world-class performers are interviewed about their success they always say the same thing, "I couldn't have done it without my parents" (my coach, my teacher, my trainer, etc.). Who's on your child's team? Who cheers him or her on? Who is willing to help? Great team members are those who share information, are willing to demonstrate support, and play to other team members' strengths. To achieve at the next level, your child must spend time with people who make her better. Think about it this week. Write it down so you can see it. Make a list of those who support your child's goals directly and indirectly.

REAL LIFE

Fifteen-year-old Kelsey won a presidential award given by a large bank to one recipient from each from the 14 high schools in her community. The award ceremony included a formal dinner in a private dining room at a five-star hotel downtown. Kelsey thoroughly enjoyed the evening and was thrilled to be included, but she would have been more comfortable had she been better prepared about what to expect.

First, there was the silverware—so many forks, knives, and spoons! What on earth were they all for? At her house there's never been more than one fork, knife, and spoon at a place setting. Kelsey wasn't sure what to do. She didn't know which silverware to use first or last, nor if she should hold on to them after she used them or leave them on her plate and let the waiter take them away. She did the best she could watching others and following their example.

There were a few foods served that were unfamiliar to her, too. She hoped that nothing would be served that she didn't like. She didn't know how she'd handle that. Meat and potatoes were the regular fare in her home.

Twice she wasn't sure sometimes whether something on her plate was a garnish or meant to be eaten. Again, she watched and followed the example of others at her table and did her best.

Most of all, Kelsey felt uncomfortable with the conversation at the table. She envied the two girls seated across from her who seemed so relaxed and natural. They made jokes and spoke freely with the others. She was interested in what they had to say, but felt tongue-tied. She found herself talking mostly with an older woman seated at the end of the table who reminded her of her grandmother.

In spite of feeling self-conscious and a bit awkward, Kelsey enjoyed herself and learned a lot from the experience. The dinner introduced her to an unfamiliar social context and gave her some insights into her background. Next time she'll be better prepared.

PRACTICAL HELP

Pianist Madeline Bruser has this to say about naysayers:

Sometimes people try to discourage you because they lack confidence themselves. They don't understand how you can dare to do what you're doing because they can't picture themselves being so daring. They may even envy you for your talent or accomplishments. If you understand these feelings, you can develop compassion for them. This doesn't mean you have to stick around while they throw darts at you; you can walk away. But you can also realize that you are richer than they are because you have more confidence. This awareness can melt your anger and open your heart for performing. (1997, p. 247)

Neighborhood or family friends may not share your child's specific interests, but they may still offer support and encouragement by asking about your his interests and expressing pleasure and pride in his progress and success. Friends who share your child's interests may offer support in practical ways like offering advice or guidance, or sharing knowledge about resources and networks.

Now consider for a moment anyone who works against your goals or your child's dreams. Is there a naysayer in your family or among your child's weekly contacts? Someone who actively discourages you or your child's efforts? Is there anyone whose questioning of your values or activities is a thorn in your side? Think for a moment and write down the names of anyone who seems to be opposing your child's efforts. Next to their names, make a note of how they oppose or discourage you or your child.

The worksheet on the next page provides you space to record your thoughts.

If you have more than two people who oppose your efforts or actively discourage you, you need to do what you can to limit your child's contact with them. High achievement is challenging enough without struggling against a lot of opposition. If it's not possible to limit that contact, then you will need to make a concerted effort to build your child's system of support to counteract it. The greater the strength of your opposition, the more you'll need a force of support on your side. It's not realistic to think that you can keep going alone. No one makes it far without a support team.

Encourage your children to surround themselves with people who will affirm their pursuit of their goals, people who endorse their aspirations. Begin by being an example for your children. They can maintain friendships with many different people, but your children will need strong relationships with selected people because strong peer groups provide the energy and emotional support needed to persevere.

People in different settings have different expectations of one another. In some learning communities people have high expectations for one another. Everyone is expected to give his or her best effort and to work hard toward a chosen goal. But, there are settings where this is not the case, where people tend to look down on those who are working hard toward some goal that others either don't understand or don't value as highly.

Your job is to help your children find others who have similar interests, abilities, and drive, and support them in spending time with these people. Do what you can to get your children into settings where they'll be encouraged to work hard at their chosen goal, where others will spur them on and motivate them by their own example. Build their team.

Just as your child may experience negative pressure for his or her success, so you as a parent also may experience your own negative peer pressure about your child's success. Family members or friends may think you're too pushy, or that you drive your child too hard, or have them involved in too much competition too early. You need to have a support team of your own—other adults who appreciate your child's achievement, motivation, and desire to excel. You'll need to

People Who Provide Direct Help

_____
_____
_____
_____
_____
_____
_____
_____

People Who Provide Indirect Help

_____
_____
_____
_____
_____
_____
_____
_____

People Who Work Against You

_____
_____
_____
_____
_____
_____
_____
_____

How They Oppose You

_____
_____
_____
_____
_____
_____
_____
_____

WORKSHEET

have at least one friend who understands and can offer a listening ear, someone with whom you can share your pleasure and pride in your child's accomplishments, as well as the occasional frustrations. Think of your supportive friends as your pit crew. Each can play an important role in keeping that great car on the track. They add fuel, renew the batteries, change the oil, fill the tires. In short, they do whatever it takes to keep the car doing the best it can.

Summary

For all of the discussion about making winners, there's little dialogue about how to help children manage success. Winning comes with a price and children must be taught how to manage it, otherwise they may eventually decide that the costs are too high and they'll settle for less than they hoped for or imagined.

Your children may have everything it takes to realize their dreams, but they may still quit if they are not prepared for the social costs of high performance and upward mobility. Frank discussions about the psychological costs of upward mobility, and about the subtle and sometimes not so subtle messages the world gives to talent will give your children permission and confidence to pursue their highest aspirations with abandon.

Chapter Resources

Arnold, K., Noble, K., & Subotnik, R. (1996). *Remarkable women: Perspectives on female talent development.* Cresskill, NJ: Hampton Press.

Bateson, M. C. (1990). *Composing a life.* New York: Penguin Books.

Bruser, M. (1997). *The art of practicing: Making music from the heart.* New York: Bell Tower.

Chambers, V. (1997). *Mama's girl.* New York: Riverhead Books.

Fleischman, P. (1999). *Weslandia.* Cambridge, MA: Candlewick Press.

From the Top. (2008, January). *Young composer honoree Todd Kramer.* Retrieved January 25, 2008, from http://www.fromthetop.org/About/PressBox.cfm?aid=574

Gabor, A. (1995). *Einstein's wife: Work and marriage in the lives of five twentieth century women.* New York: Penguin Books.

Hickam, H. (2000). *Rocket boys.* New York: Delta.

Kerr, B. (1994). *Smart girls.* Scottsdale, AZ: Great Potential Press.

McDonald, M. (1995). *Insects are my life.* New York: Orchard Books.

Obama, B. (2004). *Dreams from my father: A story of race and inheritance.* New York: Crown.

Potok, C. (1972). *My name is Asher Lev.* New York: Random House.

Suskind, R. (1998). *A hope in the unseen.* New York: Broadway Books.

Tea, M. (Ed.). (2003). *Working without a net: The female experience of growing up working class.* Emeryville, CA: Seal Books.

Walker, B. A., & Mehr, M. (1992). *The courage to achieve: Why American's brightest women struggle to fulfill their promise.* New York: Simon and Schuster.

−9−

The Most Important Thing

YOU can't expect your child to get really good at something she doesn't like.

To become an elite performer, a child must first fall in love. Romance is the most important thing.

When your child becomes totally captivated by an idea, an event, or a possibility, that's your first clue that she has the potential to reach extraordinary levels of accomplishment. She has to fall in love before she'll pursue her dreams with the kind of passion and commitment that's needed to reach the highest levels of performance.

Studies of experts of all ages tell us that people often fall in love with something after early exposure to it in the context of play. Later, as their enthusiasm persists and their desire to learn and to improve grows, they begin formal instruction with a teacher who is skilled at developing ability in children. If the romance continues and the child makes a commitment to reaching the highest levels of performance, better teachers are sought, more time is committed to developing the talent, and stakes and competition intensify. At that

 DOI: 10.4324/9781003237068-9

point, the mental and emotional skills we've talked about in this book become critical. The child who has been building these skills and mastering them along the way will have an obvious advantage over those who are just beginning.

People fall in and out of love all the time, of course. Some loves are brief fires that burn hotly and quickly, while others flame for several years. Some loves, though, last a lifetime.

When asked if she had ever considered any career besides acting, talking, or broadcasting, Oprah Winfrey (1991) said,

> I always wanted to be an actress for most of my adolescent and adult life. My father didn't want me to be, because his idea of 'an actress' was one of these 'lewd women,' and 'How are you going to take care of your life?' So I always wanted to be an actress and have taken, I think, a roundabout way to get there because I still don't feel fulfilled as an actress. I still feel like, okay, once I own my studio, but I'm thinking, I did all of this just to be an actress. I just want to be able to act. (¶ 2)

Fan the Flames of Their Passion

It doesn't matter whether your child's romance is with numbers, the French horn, or ballet, at the first sign of his passion you should begin to encourage and nurture his ability. This is the time to begin gently teaching him the emotional and mental skills he'll need to realize his dreams. Keep him moving toward his edge of competence. Set simple, yet SMART, goals. Show him how to breathe and to relax so he learns how to manage his tension. Help him to imagine the clearest picture of what he's aiming for.

Let your child pursue his dreams, not yours. Although you may have invested considerable time and resources into your child's passion, you must be willing to let it go if there comes a time when he decides to pursue something else. Your child will not find his greatest satisfaction in his work by trying to satisfy your expectations, but by doing something he feels he was destined or called to do.

In the lives of many eminent individuals, the passion for their subject matter was first kindled when they were young. As they explored their world and tried on different roles, something caught their interest and later bloomed into a romance.

E. O. Wilson, for instance, the renowned American naturalist and sociobiologist, says in his autobiography that he was interested in natural history from a very young age. Often uprooted during his early years, he had trouble sustaining friendships, and found nature to be his truest friend. Ants, in particular, have been his obsession for most of his 71 years. He's been called one of the greatest thinkers of the 20th century and has won some of the most coveted awards in science, including the U.S. National Medal of Science and the Crafoord Prize from the Royal Swedish Academy of Sciences. He also won two Pulitzer Prizes, the first in 1978 for his book, *On Human Nature*, and the second in 1990 for his tome, *The Ants*, which he cowrote with Bert Höldobler.

Some people can remember the day or season they knew, "this is for me. This is what I want to do forever." For instance, Chinese film director Andy Lau, well known for his *Infernal Affairs* trilogy, says that he was lucky a childhood friend's father was a theater manager. Although he can't recall the title of the first movie he ever saw, he can still remember what it was about. He fell in love with photography. His first job after schooling was as an assistant cinematographer, and from there he worked his way up. In 2002 his film, *Infernal Affairs*, became a box office hit, breaking several records and becoming a worldwide sensation.

In an interview with the Academy of Achievement, ABC News Correspondent Sam Donaldson said that his mother bought a radio to listen to the war news after Pearl Harbor was attacked. They had not owned a radio before that. He was 7 at the time.

> There's a picture of me at age 8 in a Cub Scout uniform holding a crystal microphone, obviously pretending that I was reading the war news. Don't ask me why I thought I wanted to do that, but I did. My mother had taught me to read, had read to me. She clearly was pushing me to try to do something with my life. And I began to read the newspaper and pretend I was reading the war news. This is the earliest known point at which something in my mind said maybe I wanted to be in the news business. But believe me, at age eight I had no idea of what the news business was like, nor did I have any feeling of the public's right to know, or the First Amendment. That would be revisionist history. I was just getting a kick out of it. (Donaldson, 1996, ¶ 6)

Oscar winning actress Whoopi Goldberg (1994), when asked when she knew what she wanted to do with her life, replied:

> "Oh, from birth. I knew as soon as I hit that light. I was waving! It's as much a part of my whole being as breathing. I always knew this was it. I didn't know it was going to be like this, you know. But I always knew that I wanted to act" (¶ 4–5).

But, for others, the journey isn't so clear, nor as direct. Ballerina Suzanne Farrell (1990) says about her childhood,

I was very much of a tomboy. So dancing was not something I had a great desire to do. In fact, ballet companies did not exist in the Midwest when I was a child. One would come to town maybe once a year. So I think it is rather strange that I got into ballet, something that I hadn't seen. But what was my motivation was music, and the fact that I love to move around. I'm always moving around. And I think it was important that I learned to love to dance eventually for its own sake, as opposed to wanting to be a ballerina. Because I think it made me realize that there was a lot of hard work involved before you get to be a ballerina. And I never lost loving the actual work that was involved in it. But then, of course, I got on stage and I decided then that I wanted to be a dancer. (¶ 2)

Olympic diver Laura Wilkinson's first love as a young girl was gymnastics, but when a growth spurt in puberty forced her out of that sport, she looked for another that she could do barefoot. Seeing a young diver execute an impressive dive one day at a pool got her interested in the sport of platform diving, and by age 18 she had joined the U.S. National Team. Now 30 years old, Laura is the only woman in history to have ever earned the gold medal in platform diving in all three world competitions.

Achieving children are distinguished by several characteristics. They have:
- high aspirations and a will to achieve,
- at least one adult who encouraged and nurtured them,
- families that tended to be optimistic and spiritual, and
- positive peer groups.

Your children already may be high performers who aren't afraid of hard work. They already may have mastered some strategies to

REAL LIFE

It was a friend's diagnosis with Cystic Fibrosis that prompted 14-year-old Madhavi Gavini to study common herbs and plants. Beginning with her grandfather's book about Indian medicinal plants, Madhavi tested common grocery store and green houseplants, such as cinnamon and ginger, for their effects on pseudomonas bacteria, a dangerous organism that causes secondary infections that are the leading cause of death in people with disorders that compromise their immune systems. Madhavi was born in India and spent a great deal of time watching her grandparents, who were practitioners of a traditional Indian healing technique called Ayurvedic medicine. She obtained a strain of pseudomonas bacteria from the local university and began subjecting the germ to various plant extracts.

Under her science teacher's tutelage, Madhavi was able to isolate the specific molecule in the extract that inhibits bacterial growth and observed that it was heat and pressure resistant. It killed the bacterium by preventing the transcription of genes.

Now 17, Madhavi has already garnered one patent, a grant from the U.S. Department of Homeland security, and more than $100,000 in awards for her discovery of this method that destroys the deadly bacterium with a combination of traditional Indian herbal medicine and molecular biology (Davidson Institute for Talent Development, n.d.).

keep a lid on their stress and are discovering ways to make rest and recovery a daily discipline. Perhaps they've recently raised the bar for themselves, or have begun competing at a new level. Maybe they've been admitted to a competitive class, school, or program, or have moved up a division in competition.

With that next step up comes a different set of demands. They may now be motivated to strengthen their ability to mentally rehearse. They may now feel the need to become more disciplined about managing their mood. They may now see more clearly the potential social costs of their success. Develop your own blueprint for what works for you and your child. Apply these techniques to your own child's situation, and take note of what helps. The worksheet on the next page is a good tool for reviewing where your child stands and what you can do to develop your blueprint for success.

Your Role

I didn't have formal acting training. I just had my mom who believed in me.

—Hillary Swank, Oscar-winning actress

Parents play a huge role in their children's performance, for better or worse. The home environment can either nurture and cultivate ability, or starve it, causing children to either abandon their efforts or to stay the course.

The road to higher levels of performance is not a straight uphill climb. It includes unexpected detours. As you nurture your children and help them to reach and realize their potential, keep in mind that they're on a developmental continuum. Develop your own blueprint of what works for your child. Apply the points that we've mentioned this week to your own situation, and take note of what helps. You are the expert on your child. Don't be overawed by those with credentials. No one knows your child like you do and no one else will love your child as you do.

Think Big, Start Small

We've covered seven essential skills your child needs to learn in order to realize his dreams. We've explored a number of strategies for developing each of them. It's not possible for you to begin with them all. Where should you start? You might use the worksheet on the next page to help you determine which areas your child needs to develop most.

Begin with the end in mind. Think big, and start small. Take inventory. What's going well? What's already in place that's working? Maybe your child has a great teacher. Perhaps he has friends who share his interests, abilities, and drive, peers who pull him along. Your child may be willing to work very hard.

What's next? Ask yourself what your child's tolerance is for stress and anxiety. If she lacks the basic skills she needs for keeping a lid on her anxiety, she will have trouble persevering through the tougher challenges ahead. Working at her edge of competence will make her apprehensive. Competitions, performances, and assessments will make her nervous. It's natural to feel fear in the face of uncertainty. Expect it. Build your child's confidence in her ability to take on a challenge by teaching her how to breathe and how to relax. Learning to manage stress and anxiety is fundamental to developing talent.

Of the seven habits that drive performance, I believe there are two that are most important. The first is essential for improving ability and the second is essential for being able to persevere.

Working at the edge of competence is a high priority. Don't let your child spend years hanging out in her comfort zone. No one gets better by continuing to play a game with people who play as well or worse than he does. No one improves by repeating what he has already mastered. Your child needs instruction that advances his ability.

Take a moment right now and consider what your child is already able to do in each of the following competencies:

Tolerating Stress and Anxiety

_____

_____

Working at the Edge of Competence

_____

_____

Goal Setting

_____

_____

Mental Rehearsal

_____

_____

Mood Management

_____

_____

Optimism

_____

_____

Managing Success

_____

_____

W O R K S H E E T

This is easier to get in some fields than in others. Music instruction, for instance, tends naturally to move children toward their edge of competence. In school bands and orchestras, in private lessons and music groups, teachers select music that builds on the child's abilities. Music teachers are careful not to overwhelm or discourage a child with a score or fingering that is too difficult.

Similarly, in fields like dance, chess, foreign language learning, sports, and the visual arts, instruction often is structured in ways that keep children with similar ability working together at their edge of competence. In competitive athletics, teams and competitions tend to be matched by ability and coaches know how to set and communicate SMART, weekly goals that advance knowledge and develop skills.

Perhaps you have access to schools that do a good job of moving your child out of his comfort zone. The curriculum is challenging, there's plenty of opportunity for your child to work with others who share his passion and ability, and the teachers provide support for realistic risks and for coping with disappointments and failure.

But, you may not. You may belong to a learning community where people are more concerned with scores or with grades than with an appropriate level of challenge. Where more effort is given to developing the ability of one group of children over developing the abilities of every child. Classroom teachers in many countries are faced with such a wide range of abilities, needs, and cultures in a single classroom that they often teach just to one group, or aim for the middle, hoping to provide a little something for everyone. As a result, most students' abilities are not optimized. Providing instruction and support that appropriately challenges every student is a daunting task for even the best teacher.

If that describes your child's situation, you will have to take a much more active role in accessing instruction for your child that moves him out of his comfort zone. I encourage you to advocate for your child and others like him—stand up and speak up, but don't wait for change to provide your child with what he or she needs to improve. Your child may get the highest marks and the best test scores, but if it requires no effort for him to do so, he's not gaining any ground. Worse, he may get the idea that he doesn't have to make an effort to succeed.

If your child is in love with numbers or technology, if he's captivated by a scientific problem, a human need, or cause, it will probably be your responsibility to connect him with others who are similar and move him out of his comfort zone toward his edge of competence.

If your child is 4 and ready to learn to read, don't wait for kindergarten. Teach him now. If your child is 7 and curious about music, arrange for lessons with a good teacher. If your child is 15 and fascinated by technology, find an accelerated summer camp, a mentor, or an advanced class at his school or local college.

To realize their dreams, your children need to learn how to make an effort, how to sustain that effort over time, how to take risks, and how to cope with the emotions that arise when setbacks and disappointments come. They won't get a chance to learn any of that if they spend all of their time sitting in their comfort zone.

Fortunately, we live in the age of technology. No matter where you live, and regardless of the age of your child, it's possible through the Internet for you to find others who share your child's passion and to locate instruction or training that's a good fit for your child.

The other priority is to develop hope and optimism. If there's one thing you can do that will build your child's resilience, keep her motivated through challenges and obstacles, and protect her from discouragement and despair, it's to build her optimism.

Just as you have been faithful to get your child the shots she needs to protect her from the debilitating effects of disease, think of optimism as a shot you can give your child that will protect her from the devastation of hopelessness and helplessness. Building optimism is simple to do and the effects last a lifetime. Begin with the basic steps we've discussed within these pages. Make it a goal to learn what your own explanatory style is like, as well as that of your children. Listen to what your children say when they face disappointment or rejection. Listen to how they explain their success. Do they take credit? Do they attribute their victories to their hard work and perseverance? Do they view themselves as growing smarter and stronger? When they're pessimistic, gently ask for the evidence that supports and doesn't support their beliefs. Ask open-ended questions that expand their ability to see multiple reasons for outcomes. Determine as a family to grow in your ability to view the reasons for your disappointments and rejections as temporary and limited, and to see the cause of your victories as enduring and pervasive.

An Encouraging Finding

It doesn't matter who you are, where you come from. The ability to triumph always begins with you. Always.

—Oprah Winfrey

One of the most provocative, yet encouraging, findings in the research on families of the highest creative producers has to do with the kinds of families they come from. Many of the eminent people we've admired over the decades did not come from child-centered, trouble-free homes. In fact, the majority of them had some kind of adversity in their upbringing: divorce, poverty, loss of a parent, illness, and the like. In other words, many (though not all) of the most creative achievers in history had family-based obstacles to surmount along the way. How do we explain this? I think the answer lies in what we know about resilience.

Circumstances don't determine outcomes. All of us know wonderful people who turned out great even though they endured terrible hardship as children. We also know people who had every advantage when they were young, yet unraveled or floundered at the first stormy wave. It's not what happens to us that determines our future, but rather, our response to what happens to us that makes the difference. The characteristics common to many talented children also are found among the characteristics of resilient people. In particular, it is widely believed that a positive explanatory style—hope and optimism—is the hallmark of resilient individuals. Because they believe that the causes of their trouble are temporary, specific, and attributable to external factors, optimistic children are hopeful and expect change. As a result, they stay motivated. They keep on trying, even in the midst of great adversity.

Finding Meaning and Purpose

It's important to remember that a sense of one's meaning and purpose often is what provides the drive for extraordinary achievement in adult life. If immediate achievements are not part of a bigger picture, sooner or later most people disengage. Everyone eventually tries to answer the question, "Why am I here?" For many of us, family offers a profound sense of meaning and purpose. For others, it's faith that gives meaning. For some, it's a cause or an idea much larger than themselves.

REAL LIFE

Do you have a high-powered teenager in your home? Then you may be able to relate to the challenges that Rudy and Peline face with their 15 year-old son, Scott.

"I worry about the pace he keeps," says Peline. "I know he's not getting enough sleep. He's rarely in bed before midnight and he's always up at 6 a.m. for swim practice. His classes are demanding. He usually has at least 2 hours of homework, and he has a part-time job. It's only 10 hours a week, and only on weekends, but still. I know he has a lot of drive, and we're proud of him, but we worry about the cost to his health and we worry about burnout. Will he even feel like going to college when the time comes? He has 3 more years of high school, 4 of college, and he'll probably want to go to grad school. He talks about earning an MBA. We hardly see him because he's gone so much, and when we do, he's often grumpy and not much fun to be around. We often wonder if all this is really necessary. What about family time? What about time to just be a kid? We worry that he's carrying too much pressure for his age."

Smart children may need to answer this question a lot earlier than other children. Why am I doing this? Why does this matter? In the big scheme of things, what difference will this make? Remember that for the most gifted children, the specific things they accomplish do not provide this profound sense of meaning. They must be able to connect what they're doing now with the larger issues of life. This need for meaning often becomes magnified during adolescence when children begin to invest more time in developing their abilities. It's hard to make the necessary sacrifices if one doesn't have a larger sense of purpose. Every child must find his or her own way, but it's your job as a parent to point him or her in that direction.

As you watch your children improve and as they grow in confidence, begin to speak to them about daily habits they can practice that will sharpen their focus and ensure a consistently outstanding performance. Especially in the teenage years, as they begin the transition from high achievement to the possibility of elite levels of performance, encourage them to make rest a discipline, to actively manage their mood, and to honestly explore the potential price of their success.

Always let your goals be SMART. Dream big dreams for your children, but don't stop there. Convert those dreams into weekly and monthly goals your children can reach and review them often with your children so that they can adjust their strategy and effort.

Teach them. Support them. Encourage them. Be their inspiration.

Summary

Nobody gets really good at something they don't like. The first step in the journey to high achievement is falling in love. Over the course of their lifetime, most children will fall in love more than once. Each romance is an opportunity to build the mental and emotional skills we've been talking about. A mother of a gifted child once told me that she viewed raising her child like taking a long bus ride. She said, "Many different people will get on and off the bus: teachers, coaches, specialists, doctors, but I'm the only one who's riding with her all the way to the end of the line." You are the expert on your child. You have what it takes to help him become the best he can be. Great achievement is open to us all.

Chapter Resources

The Academy of Achievement. (1961). Retrieved January 25, 2008, from http://www.achievement.org/autodoc/pagegen

Davidson Institute for Talent Development. (n.d.). *Davidson Fellow Laureate Madhavi Gavini.* Retrieved January 25, 2008, from http://presskit.ditd.org/2007_Davidson_Fellows_Press_Kit/2007_DFL_%20Madhavi%20Gavini.pdf

Donaldson, S. (1996). *Interview with Sam Donaldson.* Retrieved January 29, 2008, from http://www.achievement.org/autodoc/page/don0int-1

Dweck, C. (2006). *Mindset: The new psychology of success.* New York: Random House.

Farrell, S. (1990). *Ballerina of the century.* Retrieved January 25, 2008, from http://www.achievement.org/autodoc/page/far0int-1

Goldberg, W. (1994). *The one woman show.* Retrieved January 25, 2008, from http://www.achievement.org/autodoc/page/gol0int-1

Swank, H. (2007). *Memorable performances of passion and conviction.* Retrieved January 28, 2008, from http://www.achievement.org/autodoc/page/swa0int-1

Wilson, E. O. (1995). *Naturalist.* New York: Warner Books.

Winfrey, O. (1991). *America's beloved best friend.* Retrieved January 25, 2008, from http://www.achievement.org/autodoc/page/win0int-1

Answer Key

Answers to questions on pages 129–130: What They Really Say.

1. This is an optimistic response along the permanence and personalization dimensions. She attributes her failure to external factors she can do something about and she sees this weakness as temporary. She'll remedy it by going to summer camp.
2. This is a pessimistic response along the dimensions of personalization. She's not giving herself credit. She attributes her popularity to Xavier.
3. This is a pessimistic response along the personalization and permanence dimensions. He doesn't take credit for his success but attributes it to luck, which is never permanent.
4. This is an optimistic explanation along all three dimensions because she identifies specific factors that contributed to her poor performance. They are temporary and specific to this one situation.

5. This is a pessimistic explanation, especially on the dimensions of permanence and personalization. He is blaming himself and thinking he'll never be able to publish. He generalizes from this one rejection to his entire future career.

References

Bruser, M. (1997). *The art of practicing: Making music from the heart.* New York: Bell Tower.

Chambers, V. (1997). *Mama's girl.* New York: Riverhead Books.

Davidson Institute for Talent Development. (n.d.). *Davidson Fellow Laureate Madhavi Gavini.* Retrieved January 25, 2008, from http://presskit.ditd.org/2007_Davidson_Fellows_Press_Kit/2007_DFL_%20Madhavi%20Gavini.pdf

Donaldson, S. (1996). *Interview with Sam Donaldson.* Retrieved January 29, 2008, from http://www.achievement.org/autodoc/page/don0int-1

Engelland, A. (2006, November 21). Getting the buzz on caffeine. *The Larchmont Gazette*, ¶ 9–15. Retrieved January 29, 2008, from http://www.larchmontgazette.com/2006/teenhealth/index.html

Ericsson, K. A. (2002). Attaining excellence through deliberate practice: Insights from the study of expert performance. In M. Ferrari (Ed.), *The pursuit of excellence through education* (pp. 21–56). London: Lawrence Erlbaum.

Farrell, S. (1990). *Ballerina of the century.* Retrieved January 25, 2008, from http://www.achievement.org/autodoc/page/far0int-1

Fleischman, P. (1999). *Weslandia.* Cambridge, MA: Candlewick Press.

From the Top. (2008, January). *Young composer honoree Todd Kramer.* Retrieved January 25, 2008, from http://www.fromthetop.org/About/PressBox.cfm?aid=574

Goldberg, W. (1994). *The one woman show.* Retrieved January 25, 2008, from http://www.achievement.org/autodoc/page/gol0int-1

Hickam, H. (2000). *Rocket boys.* New York: Delta.

McDonald, M. (1995). *Insects are my life.* New York: Orchard Books.

Potok, C. (1972). *My name is Asher Lev.* New York: Random House.

Suskind, R. (1998). *A hope in the unseen.* New York: Broadway Books.

Stickgold, R. (2005). Sleep-dependent memory consolidation. *Nature, 437,* 1272–1278.

Ungerleider, S. (2005). *Mental training for peak performance.* New York: Rodale.

Winfrey, O. (1991). *America's beloved best friend.* Retrieved January 25, 2008, from http://www.achievement.org/autodoc/page/win0int-1

Selected Research on Peak Performance

Beilock, S., & Carr, T. (2005).When high-powered people fail: Working memory and "choking under pressure" in math. *Psychological Science, 16,* 101–105.

Bloom, B. (Ed.). (1985). *Developing talent in young people.* New York: Ballantine.

Bryan, J., & Locke, E. (1967). Goal setting as a means of increasing motivation. *Journal of Applied Psychology, 51,* 274–277.

Clifford, M., Lan, W., Chou, F., & Q-I, Y. (1989). Academic risk-taking: Developmental and cross cultural observations. *Journal of Experimental Education, 57,* 321–338.

Csikszentmihalyi, M., Rathunde, K., & Whalen, S. (1993). *Talented teenagers: Roots of success and failure.* New York: Cambridge University Press.

Duckworth, A. I., & Seligman, M. (2005). Self-discipline outdoes IQ in predicting academic performance. *Psychological Science, 16,* 939–944.

Dweck, C. S. (1986). Motivational processes affecting learning. *American Psychologist, 41,* 1040–1048.

Ericsson, K. A. (1998). The scientific study of expert levels of performance: General implications for optimal learning and creativity, *High Ability Studies, 9,* 75–100.

Ericsson, K. A., Krampe, R. T., & Tesch-Romer, C. (1993). The role of deliberate practice in the acquisition of expert performance. *Psychological Review, 100,* 363–406.

Farmer, H. S. (1976). What inhibits achievement and career motivation in women? *The Counseling Psychologist, 6,* 12–14.

Grant, H., & Dweck, C. (2003). Clarifying achievement goals and their impact. *Journal of Personality and Social Psychology, 85,* 541–553.

Hanin, Y. L. (1997). Emotions and athletic performance: Individual zones of optimal functioning model. *European Yearbook of Sport Psychology, 1,* 29–72.

Hollenbeck, J., Williams, C., & Klein, H. (1989). An empirical examination of the antecedents of commitment to difficult goals. *Journal of Applied Psychology, 74,* 8–23.

Horvat, E. M., & Lewis, K. S. (2003). Reassessing the "burden of acting White": The importance of peer groups in managing academic success. *Sociology of Education, 76,* 265–280.

Jones, G., Hanton, S., & Swain, A. B. J. (1994). Intensity and interpretation of anxiety symptoms in elite and non-elite sports performers. *Personal Individual Differences, 17,* 657–663.

Kammins, M. L., & Dweck, C. S. (1999). Person versus process praise and criticism: Implications for contingent self-worth and coping. *Developmental Psychology, 35,* 835–847.

Kellogg, J. S., Hopko, D. R., & Ashcraft, M. H. (1999). The effects of time pressure in arithmetic performance. *Journal of Anxiety Disorders, 13,* 591–600.

Latham, G. P., & Kinne, S. B. (1974). Improving job performance through training in goal setting. *Journal of Applied Psychology, 59,* 187–191.

Mallett, C. J., & Hanrahan, S. J. (2004). Elite athletes: Why does the "fire" burn so brightly? *Psychology of Sport and Exercise, 5,* 183–200.

McClelland, D. C. (1963). The calculated risk: An aspect of scientific performance. In C. W. Taylor & F. Barron (Eds.), *Scientific creativity: Its recognition and development* (pp. 184–192). New York: John Wiley & Sons.

Osborne, J. (1997). Race and academic disidentification. *Journal of Educational Psychology, 89,* 728–735.

Ostrove, J. M. (2003). Belonging and wanting: Meanings of social class background for women's constructions of their college experiences. *Journal of Social Issues, 59,* 771–784.

Peters, H. J., & Williams, J. M. (2006). Moving cultural background to the foreground: An investigation of self-talk, performance, and persistence following feedback. *Journal of Applied Sport Psychology, 18,* 240–253.

Peterson, C., & Barrett, L. (1987). Explanatory style and academic performance among university freshman. *Journal of Personality and Social Psychology, 17,* 114–124.

Randle, S., & Weinberg, R. (1997). Multidimensional anxiety and performance: An exploratory examination of the zone of optimal functioning hypothesis. *The Sport Psychologist, 11,* 160–174.

Reis, S. M., & Callahan, C. M. (1996). My boyfriend, my girlfriend, or me: The dilemma of talented teenage girls. *Journal of Secondary Gifted Education, 2,* 434–446.

Seligman, M., Nolen-Hoeksema, S., Thornton, N., & Thornton, K. M. (1990). Explanatory style as a mechanism of disappointing athletic performance. *Psychological Science, 1,* 143–146.

Subotnik, R. F., & Arnold, K. D. (1996). Success and sacrifice: The costs of talent fulfillment for women in science. In K. Arnold, K. Noble, & R. Subotnik (Eds.), *Remarkable women: New per-*

spectives on female talent development (pp. 263–280). Cresskill, NJ: Hampton Press.

Thelwell, R. C., Greenlees, I. A., & Weston, N. J. V. (2006). Using psychological skills training to develop soccer performance. *Journal of Applied Sport Psychology, 18,* 254–270.

About the Author

MAUREEN Neihart is a licensed child psychologist with more than 25 years of experience working with talented young people and their families. A former teacher and school counselor, she now is an internationally recognized leader on the psychological aspects of children's talent development. An energizing speaker, Dr. Neihart is a frequent presenter at state and national conferences throughout the U.S. and also addresses international audiences in Europe, Asia, and South America.

Dr. Neihart is a long-time advocate for talented children and their families. She has shown a keen interest in children's development since she ran a day camp for preschoolers when she was 10 years old. Volunteer experiences in high school and college awakened her passion for helping others realize their potential and inspired her to become a secondary teacher. The opportunities she had to help youth from all walks of life pursue their dreams energized her to pursue a doctoral degree in counseling psychology. Later, as a child psychologist, she coached youth and families to help them learn how to overcome their fears and make the most of their abilities.

Dr. Neihart is coeditor of the popular text, *The Social and Emotional Development of Gifted Children: What Do We Know?*, and also serves on the editorial boards of several journals. Her articles often appear in state, regional, and national newsletters and magazines. Among her writing credits, Dr. Neihart is especially proud of her one act comedy, *The Court Martial of George Armstrong Custer*, which was produced and filmed for local television in 2000.

In 2006, Dr. Neihart moved with her husband Doug, a high school administrator, to Singapore, where she is Associate Professor of Psychological Studies at the National Institute of Education.